MORE THAN A DOG'S TALE

A Life With Dogs and Other Animals

a memoir by

LINDA MACK

Copyright © 2019 by Linda Mack
All rights reserved.
ISBN: 978-1-950186-11-2

Book Design and Layout by Jennifer Leigh Selig
Cover Image Credits—End of Book

AUTHOR'S DISCLAIMER

The stories in this book are true, to the best of my recollection. Memory is almost always flawed, but I've written details as I remember them, as they reside in my head, and if mistakes have been made, don't blame my intent. Blame my imperfect memory. These are stories of real people, real animals, and actual events. Conversations are not verbatim. I hope they catch the temper of events that occurred. Some names have been changed and some descriptions slightly altered to protect the privacy of some individuals.

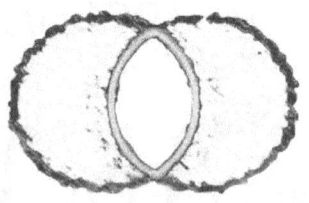

MANDORLA BOOKS
WWW.MANDORLABOOKS.COM

DEDICATION

To Marcella Lorfing, who left this earth too soon, in gratitude for the push that got me started. And to Kit Kirkpatrick whose encouragement, generosity and energy have inspired me to keep going.

And to Ralfie.

TABLE OF CONTENTS

	Introduction	1
1	The Pigeon on the Porch	7
2	Animal Control Officer One	15
3	Chester	21
4	Dogs as Family	29
5	Boulou	35
6	An Unavoidable Side Effect	39
7	Mrs. Calabash	43
8	A Singular Pit Bull	47
9	English Setters Against Angst	53
10	Michael and the Cannons	69
11	Romar Kennels	77
12	Here Kitty Kitty	91
13	My Mother	97
14	Buster Bean and Midge, Et Al.	107
15	Just Dog	115
16	Little Brothers	119
17	On Being a Hero	127
18	Bran Flakes	135
19	Hal	139
20	Bert and Carl	142
21	Franky	149

22	A Monkey	159
23	Janet and Rupert	165
24	The Big Sheep	175
25	Spike	181
26	Luna Flor	191
27	Always a Downside	195
28	The Prison Pet Partnership Program at Purdy	203
	Epilogue	207
	About the Author	209
	Image Credits	211

INTRODUCTION

On January 21, 2018, my 15-year-old long-haired Chihuahua, Lily (a sweet, smart, beautiful little animal and good friend), passed away. She had been failing for some time with common maladies of old age—arthritis, bad knees, bad kidneys—but until that day in January she still had a little wag in her. When she stopped eating, she had nothing more to wag about except for the slight flutter she still managed when I touched her. Her refusal of roast chicken, her favorite food, was the sign that she was ready to go. The decision to have her euthanized was based on my belief in the Golden Rule. "Do unto others as you would have others do unto you" is an easy rule to understand. Versions of it are found in many other cultures older than our own. Someone figured out a long time ago that it's a good rule to follow if you want a good life. I try to follow it, as well as another more difficult rule, "Do unto myself as I would have others do unto me." Working on following the second rule has required some years of therapy, along with years of associating with dogs and other animals. I'm still working on getting those rules down to a science. It's a practice that passes for my religion, I guess, in lieu of any other.

Many people are sure that dogs and cats don't live long enough. When a beloved pet dies, they vow never to get another. I couldn't do that, although I used to concur with the belief that dogs and cats don't live long enough. I tolerated the situation because I can't imagine living without a dog or two (or more) in my life, despite the grief and heartache at the end. However, I heard something the other day that I will remember and appreciate. A little girl was asked why she thought dogs live such a short life compared to humans. She said that humans were put on the Earth to learn how to be honest and generous and how to love unconditionally. Dogs take less time to learn all that, so they can leave sooner. I like that idea, no matter its overly sugary sweetness. Like at the end of a Hallmark movie, I may roll my eyes, but some truth in there gives me a reason to smile.

My friend and partner, Charlene, and I took Lily to the only vet in our single-stop-light small town. Dr. Bear is a slightly rumpled, ex-Marine, ex-hippy. He wears sandals with socks, and he has a brisk, no nonsense crew-cut. Everyone assumes that his politics align with their own, and in this small-town, political factions are sharply divided. No one believes Dr. Bear favors the "other side." He's always on our side, whoever we happen to be.

Dr. Bear treats animals large and small in our farming community. When we took Lily to him, he knew exactly what we needed and what we needed to hear. We were shown to a comfortable room with two chairs. I sat down with Lily snuggled on my chest. Charlene sat next to me, quietly telling Lily a nice, if tearful, tale about going away, "And you'll be able to bounce and jump and shake that little blue piggy again....." I always hope those kinds of stories are true, even if I think they're silly. Little Lily was always a true believer. She didn't understand a word (except *sit, down, dance, turn-around* and *sneeze*), but she was willing to let it all be gospel if it came from one of her people.

Dr. Bear put two fingers lightly on Lily's head. "I'm going to prepare her shot now. Say your last good-byes."

INTRODUCTION

He was gone for about 10 minutes while we cried and came to terms with what was about to happen. When he came back, he knelt next to me to administer the injection with a gentle, careful touch. "It'll take a few minutes. I'll be back shortly." He went out of the room again, long enough for Lily to expire peacefully in my arms. When he returned this time, he had a bottle of Wild Turkey and three shot glasses. "We also have Pepsi if you prefer." Charlene chose Pepsi. He poured us each half a shot and raised his glass for a toast, "To Lily. Dogs are God's unquestioning love on earth. That's why 'dog' is 'god' spelled backwards." All three of us were smiling with tears in our eyes. Charlene and I left with the little bundle that used to be Lily. By the time we got to the car, we were laughing, which is not incompatible with profound sadness.

Lily was going to be the last of my life-long line of dog associates. "In my retirement years," I used to say, "I don't want to be tied down to an animal. I want to do some unencumbered traveling."

Lily was not my last dog, of course. In spite of what I tried to tell myself, Ralfie came home with me the following April. His previous owner, a neighbor of mine, put an ad in our neighborhood paper that a Toy Australian Shepherd needed a new home. I just wanted to know what a Toy Australian Shepherd looked like (I said to myself), and he was only a five-minute walk from my house. I went to take a look. The dog looked like a tiny (12 pounds) black and tan Australian Shepherd, cutest little animal you can imagine. He curved himself into a happy C-shape in lieu of wagging the tail he didn't have.

My neighbor was diagnosed with stage four lung cancer five years before I met him. He was given less than a year to live back then, but he has medicine dogs. He had two of them already when he accepted Ralfie from another neighbor who was moving to a dog-free living situation. Three dogs were too much for him, but I had none, so I took Ralfie home with me. He is a handful. He has the excess energy of his breed. We have been to obedience classes, where he excels. Outside of class and out of doors, he is willful, stubborn and easily distracted. He barks maniacally at other dogs on leashes, disregarding commands, pleas, water sprayed from a bottle, a buzzing collar.... He likes other dogs if he and they are not on leashes, but that isn't an option when we're walking around the neighborhood, which we do once or twice a day. We are frequently re-routed to avoid causing a major ruckus. He's perfectly behaved in the house, however, and he's better than any number of pills at keeping me calm, healthy, happy and entertained. He may be a little neurotic, but so am I, and so are most of my favorite people. His one drooping ear gives him a charm that is totally irresistible.

I'm mostly a "dog person." According to some, the world is divided into "dog people," "cat people," and people who don't like animals at all, but I'm a cat person, too. I think it more likely that there are people who like animals a lot and people who just don't get it. I'm one who loves most animals more than I care for most members of my own species. This is a memoir about my life with animals (mostly dogs), my family and my job as a City of Seattle Animal Control Officer in the 1980s. Writing about animals and about working for Animal Control has been the best retirement project imaginable. When I

INTRODUCTION

travel, Ralfie is a fine traveling companion and a bridge to conversations with people I would otherwise never meet—as long as those people don't have dogs on leashes with them.

CHAPTER 1

THE PIGEON ON THE PORCH

Pigeons are ordinary, most of them, but even the most ordinary of pigeons can have a profound effect on a human life—mine, as an example. All animals have something to admire, teach, share or give—even humans. The pigeon in this story gave me a couple of things, the first being a challenge. Although she was as lacking in intellectual acuity as most of her kind, she also instigated a radical change in my life that had been brewing since before I could remember. Her predicament ultimately illuminated for me the answer to the important question: What do I want to be when I grow up? I was already over 30, so the revelation was a long time coming.

The pigeon was pigeon-pretty, with a forest-green vest of tiny sequins over velvet gray. For more than two hours she flapped and fumbled back and forth across my mostly enclosed front porch, which was about 20 feet long and six feet deep across the front of the house. The porch had a wide opening above the wide steps leading up to it. She had plenty of room to fly away but she refused to make that crucial turn. I tried to urge her in the right direction with a broom, but she only became more agitated. She stepped up the pace and a splat of white goo appeared on the floor of my previously pristine porch. After one splat I felt sorry for her—maybe a little irritated. She continued bashing her head and splatted some more as she flew back and forth across the porch and I became sorrier for her, scared for her, and way more irritated.

Leaving the pigeon alone to figure it out was a waste of time. She couldn't figure it out. I went in the house for half an hour to give her the chance. When I came back, she was still there. I tried herding her with other things— a big piece of cardboard, the snow shovel, a bigger broom…. Her inferred reply was a definite NO to all offers of assistance. She refused my help, ducking and evading and continuing to be oblivious to the wide, sunny opening to freedom. Sometimes she sat and rested on the bench at the far end of the porch between efforts, but she began her self-bashing again whenever I moved to offer help.

At the time the pigeon arrived in my life I was trying to get on a track that would lead to somewhere, but paths and destinations were hidden from me. I was meandering, picking up interesting curiosities along the way but going nowhere. I had been attending the University of Washington (UW), taking classes that were interesting or fun, all paid for by veterans' benefits, which I vowed to use up to the last penny. No single career or profession appealed. I yearned to follow some destiny, but no matter how hard I tried, I could not force one into being.

My chosen classes had no particular goal except enjoyment (tinged with a little bit of revenge). I loved— love—learning. Teaching, though, wasn't a good fit for me. The thought of standing in front of a group of people who were waiting for me to say something was terrifying. I prefer people one at a time or in very small groups, and I much prefer adults to children—and animals to most humans. Teaching adults was out of the question while I still felt more like an adolescent. Also, NO to nursing, NO to being a secretary, NO to waitressing, NO to cooking (I was a bad, terrible, inexperienced, uninterested cook), NO to sciences, due to the involvement of calculus, chemistry and physics.

At some things I was competent enough, but most of my skills required a slow, thoughtful approach. I never have operated satisfactorily at high speeds. Employers wanted speed and efficiency—not me. I was good at writing journals and school papers, meditating, art classes, conversation, thinking about how things and people and animals operate in the world.... Thinking about calculus, chemistry and physics was enjoyable, although doing the mental gymnastics involved in making them operate as intended gave me grief. None of the decent paying jobs in my cloudy line of sight seemed sustainable on a daily basis.

The Navy had booted me from its ranks a few years before the pigeon came along. I was discharged for being gay when I was in my last year as a Midshipman at the UW. That was in 1976. I had been in the Navy for five years, three of those attending college under the "Navy Enlisted Scientific Education Program." Test scores qualified me for the prestigious program. That was another thing I was good at—taking tests.

My "General Discharge Under Honorable Conditions," allowed me to retain eligibility for benefits. With 20 more credits I could have qualified for a BS degree in Geological Oceanography. I had chosen that major from a limited list of sciences offered by the Navy's program. None sparked a thrill. Geological oceanography stood out for its location more than anything else—The University of Washington. Wow, to be an alumnus of such an awesome college! However, up to the day I left the Navy, geological oceanography remained a foreign country to me and not one of the friendly ones. After navigating some seriously rough terrain—the aforementioned calculus, chemistry and physics classes along with a few related horrors, I was happy to be rid of my science major. Getting those 20 additional credits wasn't worth the misery, especially since I was no longer the property of the U.S. Navy. With my benefits I continued taking classes, but only the fun, interesting ones.

I thought at the beginning of my college career that I would be happy attending any and all classes at the beautiful U-dub, no matter what subjects my Navy-given scientific major required. LOL.

After the pigeon had been thumping her little head on the walls and ceiling of the porch for a couple of hours, an idea came to me—Animal Control. A pigeon is an animal. If any animal needed controlling, it was that bird. I called to see if Animal Control might help me with the problem. The person who answered the call said, "Sure, we'll send someone out. There's an officer in your neighborhood right now." Hallelujah.

The officer who showed up within ten minutes turned out to be someone I knew. I hadn't seen Becky for a long time and didn't know her well, but I was overjoyed to see a familiar, kind face. I knew she would be gentle with my unwelcome guest. By that time, I had developed a sympathetic relationship with the pigeon, annoying as she was.

Officer Becky solved the problem with elegant simplicity. She tossed a small, light blanket over the tired bird, gathered her up and then carefully unwrapped her into freedom. Too easy. I could have done that. I should have done that and saved the pretty pigeon the headache she must have had by the time she flew away. I asked, "How did you know to do that?"

"That wasn't my first pigeon." She laughed. "Some things you learn from experience in this job."

"Do you like your job?" I was thinking how nice it would be to have a job where I could wear a uniform. Becky's brown uniform looked sharp, and she was wearing a silver badge, like a real police officer's. Cool. I'd never have to buy another dress....

"It's a pretty good job. Some parts aren't that great, but pay and benefits aren't bad. I get to drive around the city and do something new every day. It isn't boring, but I'm not planning to stay with it. I'm saving up to go to Clown School in Florida."

"Clown School? That's a new one. I'm looking for a job but Clown School doesn't sound like fun to me. Your job sounds like more fun."

"I think being a clown is going to be more fun and more me than doing this is." The radio attached to her belt beeped. "Oops, I'd better go. I have more calls to get to. Maybe we can get together and catch up some time. Nice to see you again."

"Yeah. We should get together sometime. Thanks for saving my pigeon-friend."

"No problem. Hey, Animal Control usually has jobs open. People are always coming and going. You should apply." Becky's radio beeped again and she pulled it out of its holster.

"Okay, okay, I'm on my way. 10-4...." She bounced down the steps. "Gotta scoot. Bye." I wondered where she was needed in such a hurry, what was her next adventure?

As I watched Becky hop into her truck, a funny feeling started in my chest making me tingle all over. I felt like crying or laughing or both. Animals! I could work with animals again! Dogs practically raised me, and I had genuine paid work experience with them. They were my people. If it hadn't been too late in the day, I would have raced down to the city employment office right then.

Perfect! Dogs were (and continue to be) so important in my life. They have always been family and have always been there for me. Fate sent that pigeon to my porch. She suffered so that I could be employed. Bless the pigeon. I knew without a doubt that I wanted to be an Animal Control Officer—a dog-catcher, a pigeon saver—and whatever else might be required of me. Dogs. I could work again with dogs, with animals—lovely beasts. Why hadn't I thought of going to the dogs before? They were a theme in my life.

The next day, early, I went to the city employment office. I had already applied for several jobs there, but I lacked the explicit qualifications for most of the available posts—and I hadn't the confidence to sell/spin the qualifications I did have. The job of Animal Control Officer had no openings available but I asked for an application anyway. The clerk said, as I started to fill out the paperwork, "You want to be a dog-catcher? That's crazy." After I handed her the completed application, she administered the test I needed to pass as part of the application process. My score put me at the top of the list for the next open position.

My experience working with animals included grooming English Setters (my high-school job) and working at Romar Kennels in California, pre-Navy. This was the first application where I had something substantial and relevant to list under "Work Experience."

As I was leaving the city employment office, the clerk tried to dampen my enthusiasm again. "That job is real stressful. Some people don't last two weeks. They don't know what they're gettin' into." Neither did I, but I knew my path had opened up. I made that crucial turn. Besides working with animals, driving around my favorite city, doing something new and different every day, I had all the confidence in the world that I could actually do the work. Here was a direction, a focus, something I wanted to do, something having to do with my favorite family. Dogs and cats, pigeons and rats, raccoons and bats.... Who knew what other creatures might need help out there. I owed them.

My associations with animals had always made it possible for me to live my life in reasonably good humor. I had no idea how much the job would shade my humor and expand my life-experience. The good always outweighed the bad. I have never regretted the nine years I spent working Animal Control. *"Thank you, Pigeon!"*

CHAPTER 2

ANIMAL CONTROL OFFICER ONE

Nine months after submitting my application—when I had nearly given up hope and was about to take a job with the city's water department—Animal Control called me for an interview. Finally! I had no doubts at all that I would sail through the interview and land my job as an Animal Control Officer.

The day after the interview I received a call offering me the job of Animal Control Officer One, also known as Kennel Attendant. For a minute or two I was crushed. I wanted to be saving animals out in the world, not tending them in the kennel. I had done that kind of work already. Scrubbing kennels was neither a challenge nor an adventure. I wanted to be on the next level.

Some of the questions the interviewers posed the day before had shaken me a bit, but I left the interview with my confidence intact. I knew the job wasn't all bright lights and happy puppies, but the interviewers' dose of reality did nothing but give the work dimension, coupled with a large dose of fear, although not enough fear to change my mind. Being slapped hard with reality didn't cause me to change my mind.

The woman on the phone, the kindliest one of my inquisitors from the previous day, explained that two years as a kennel attendant would qualify me for a promotion to field officer—Animal Control Officer Two. No one hired on as a field officer, unless they had at least a year of experience as a field officer, or the equivalent. She went on to say that several qualified candidates were considered for the open position, but my answer to one difficult question put me way ahead of the others. The question—one that I had not anticipated—was, "How will you cope with assisting a vet with the daily euthanizing of animals?" I had no idea how I could possibly do that. My brain went numb. The concept of helping to kill animals was gut-wrenching and heartbreaking, deep in the realm of denial, where most sensible people let it be.... *Was assisting the vet with this wretched task part of the job?* I coveted the job, whatever the cost, even this. I knew the job was already mine, so I dove into the ice with the answer, "I imagine I'll cry at first, but I can handle it." My answer was the kind of answer they were looking for. As it turned out, my answer was the truth, much to my relief—and much to my disappointment.

The woman on the phone said, "Do you want the job? You can start on Monday if the answer is yes."

If being a kennel attendant was a necessary first step, so be it. "Yes. I can start on Monday."

"Ask for Jay. I'll do your orientation and get you set up for uniforms."

Becky failed to mention the fact that I would have to work in the kennels before being allowed to do what she was doing. The job I applied for wasn't the job I thought I was applying for, but I still got to wear the uniform. The badge would have to come later.

By the time I hired on, Becky had already left for Clown School. I should have followed through on her offer to get together. We could have discussed a few of the details. The bloom on my dream job shriveled a bit after the initial interview, but acceptance settled in quickly. I was on a path carved out for me. I'd already scrubbed my fair share of dog kennels. I knew that the exercise would be good for me. Everything good has to be balanced with a certain amount of not-so-good. All right then. *I can do this.*

Hanging out with dogs was the thing I had done always and forever. They would keep me cheerful and on track. My duties as a kennel attendant, besides assisting the vet with euthanasia and cleaning kennels, included care and feeding of the animals, checking in and assessing the adoptability of the pets surrendered (for a $5.00 fee) or animals dumped anonymously at the shelter. I would also be handling adoptions.

Far too few members of the public adopted the available animals, which made the heartbreaking task with the vet in the back room all the more heartbreaking. A room at the front of the shelter stayed open for drop-offs after hours. Dog and cat cages were provided in the receiving room, but some people persisted in tying animals to shrubs in front of the building or leaving them in boxes outside the unlocked door. Another of my daily activities involved trying to educate the pet-seeking public about the duties and responsibilities of pet ownership, a completely thankless, useless effort when dealing with enthusiastic pet-seekers, humans who assumed owning a pet was a natural entitlement, and not a life-changing decision that required instructions and cautions.

Day-to-day duties as a kennel attendant were not always exciting, although being surrounded by animals every day was a joy. Animals are amazing, fascinating, animated works of art. Interacting with so many of them every day was sublime, most of the time. Working in the kennels gave me experience with a variety of animals besides dogs—cats, ferrets, goats, rabbits, parrots, chickens, pigs, reptiles. All kinds of animals came into the shelter, either surrendered or picked up as strays.

Helping the veterinarian with the euthanizing of surplus animals required removing myself from myself, numbing mind and emotions, but I managed to cope. The necessity fed an antipathy I had for the masses of humanity who thoughtlessly caused the pet-population explosion. I felt especially angry because I understood the mind-set that allowed people to ignore what they/we were doing to the animals. Knowing that I would eventually get out of the shelter and into the field gave me something to look forward to—an end to my part in the horrific task in the back room. I would still have to deal with the public, but with the badge, I could at least write tickets for some of the public's irresponsible behavior toward their pets.

Miserable as it was, the up-close exposure to the processes of death changed and strengthened me. The first animal I held for the veterinarian's needle was a four or five-month-old puppy, a golden brown hyper-active, happy little animal. I will never forget him. I cried. The somber vet ignored my tears and showed me how to hold the pup; how to find the vein on his front leg; how to rotate the vein and squeeze a little so the needle would slide in quickly and efficiently. I tried to keep from crying too much because I needed to hold the puppy still in order for the kill-shot to be swift and effective, with a minimum of stress to the animal. The needle slid into his vein. Within seconds, the little dog had collapsed in my arms. In less than a minute, I felt his life leave him. I had not expected to feel that. His body became empty of life. The stethoscope confirmed he was gone, and I was free to let go and sob. I suddenly had a new perspective on the concept of a soul. The puppy was gone, really gone, when I laid his little empty body down and went to fetch the next animal. The possibility that the puppy went somewhere made sense to me for the first time. I really wanted that puppy's spirit to have gone somewhere. I decided not to overthink the experience and let it be.

That pigeon—cousin of those white doves that show up in religious experiences—sent me to a place where life and death and tragedy and reconciliation and sadness and happiness and so many other dramatic vignettes showed up virtually every day, sometimes in miniature, and sometimes larger than life. Who knew that working in an Animal Control shelter came with its own version of a spiritual path? Don't look for religion in this paragraph. I still don't do that, but I think that finding a right job at a right time can be similar to a religious experience.

CHAPTER 3

CHESTER

When I began my work at Seattle Animal Control as a kennel attendant, a new animal shelter and spay/neuter clinic were under construction. Temporarily, the animal shelter was situated in a modified warehouse about a mile south of the construction site. As a new recruit, I was introduced slowly to the whole of my duties while getting used to the more unpleasant tasks, the worst of which was helping to kill surplus animals.

Finding the strength to assist the veterinarian was extremely difficult, but I learned to perform the task day after day. The justification for killing the animals made sense, but it didn't make the task any easier. "Killing" is what we did—as humanely as possible—but killing is the most direct word, even though "euthanizing" sounds less harsh. I always had a hard time thinking of any animal as "surplus." However, no one had the means to take responsibility for the surplus animals. Resources for caring for them were limited. Letting them run loose was more cruel than killing them. Domestic pets can't easily fend for themselves. If they manage to survive, they can become a danger to the public and to other animals, by spreading disease, becoming aggressive, competing for food. The job of killing had to be done.

Working in the shelter I saw what happened to

abandoned animals. I saw how many came to the shelter every single day. The shelter was overcrowded from day one, and the problem wasn't going away any time soon. It's still a problem. Steps can be taken to slow the ongoing disaster, but pet-proliferation keeps out-pacing the steps and good intentions. Still, I continued to love the job—making new friends and learning something new almost every hour of every day.

As a respite from the gritty work in the kennel and back rooms of the shelter, I was often assigned to work in the front office, greeting people, checking in animals, answering questions. The front office was the place where I was privileged to enjoy the company of Chester, the shelter cat. His tattered ears and scarred face told of a challenging previous life, but he carried himself with the gravity of an old English butler. When we first met, he acknowledged me briefly and then took up his position in the out-going mail tray on the counter that separated the office from the visiting public.

Chester's friendship was another confirmation that I was in the right place at the right time. He came to live permanently at the shelter shortly before I began working there, but his story had already become legend. The story told of how he walked—or rather staggered—into the receiving area on his own, unaccompanied, in the middle of the day. Some member of the public opened the door for him and said loudly, "OhMyGod! There's a cat out here and you people need to do something about it right NOW!" The person or persons who let the ragged orange cat inside were apparently so repulsed by the cat's condition that they turned around and left.

Chester was obviously a stray in trouble. His faded pinkish fur matted in clumps surrounded by patches of inflamed skin. He had a torn ear and his tail had been partially severed. The wounded tail was infected. The wreck-of-a-cat reeked of gangrene and filth. Ordinarily an animal in the shape he was in would be euthanized immediately, but this one had come to the shelter on his own, asking for help. He purred when one of the staff wrapped him in a towel and picked him up. The sonorous purr saved his life. Someone in authority made the decision, as the purr rumbled, to allow the cat to be taken to the vet. This was the same veterinarian who did euthanasia for the shelter. He was a kind, caring animal doctor with an office nearby. The doctor agreed to treat the ruined cat for free after hearing that the cat had surrendered himself to the shelter. Chester was the first and only animal known to surrender himself to the shelter. Nearly everybody felt he deserved a chance.

The vet shaved the cat down to the skin and amputated half of his tail. Fluids were given intravenously. Then began a round of antibiotics. The cat came to be known as Chester. Food had to be introduced gradually because he hadn't eaten anything for a long time. At first the vet thought he had maybe a 50/50 chance of surviving. Hourly bulletins kept the shelter staff informed of his condition for the first few days. Everyone celebrated when the doctor said that Chester looked as if he might recover. Several of the shelter employees visited the cat on their breaks and everyone knew how his recovery progressed in detail, from day to day.

No one took credit for naming the cat Chester. Neither the vet nor any of his technicians nor his office manager could say how the patient came to be called Chester. "Maybe he named himself," they suggested.

Chester watched, napped, or accepted friendly pats and ear-scratches by passers-by. When conditions were right, he treated us to his rumbling purr, which could be heard across the room. Sometimes he roused himself for a stretch or a snack or to patrol the office. Few things bothered him. Loud noises didn't faze him. He didn't perceive dogs as a threat. People were usually acknowledged with polite detachment.

A sign taped below the mail tray said "Please do not disturb the cat." Most people didn't read the sign and those who did often seemed to take it as an invitation to pay particular attention to the cat. Chester was accommodating. He occasionally rumbled for them when certain people treated him nicely, but if anyone became too personal or bothersome, he took himself out of sight behind the counter. Even with grabby children, he was as respectful as they allowed him to be before he slipped behind the counter. There he made himself comfortable on a desktop below the counter overhang, out of sight and out of reach, until the irritant moved on.

Dogs sometimes barked at Chester, but usually dogs were unaware of him, as he sat like an orange sphinx in his mail-tray. A dog had to be exceptionally rowdy to bother the self-possessed cat enough to make him retreat. As soon as the unpleasantness was over, he hopped back up on the counter and into his tray. The displaced outgoing paper mail sat in a stack next to the tray. The mail carrier always came with a treat for the cat, with whom he felt a certain kinship. Chester and he were colleagues of a sort, both with jobs relating to the U.S. mail. Eventually, the temporary shelter received a locking mailbox on the outside of the building, but the mail carrier continued to come inside to pay his respects.

Chester wasn't a young cat, but his true age was hard to guess because of his condition. His bad teeth indicated he was well past middle age, but given his general condition, bad teeth may have been worsened as the result of a rough diet. Several of his teeth had to be pulled. His claws had been removed before he came to the shelter, giving him a serious disadvantage living outside on his own. He was a survivor. He had to be one smart kitty to stay alive without claws.

The vet, his technicians, most of the shelter staff, friends and family were all invested in the well-being of the self-surrendered cat. Over a period of weeks, Chester began to require less monitoring. The infection receded. The bandage came off his tail, now shortened to about five or six inches. He was eating well. His hair had grown out a little. He was a long-haired cat and still needed more of his coat to grow back when he was released from care. On his release, he had a choppy, punk hair-cut over his entire body and a large scab at the end of his short tail. The vet couldn't keep him at the clinic any longer, but the recovering cat needed some rehab time before he would be ready for adoption. A couple of people tried taking him home to foster, but Chester did not like other cats and had a few other annoying habits that made him a less than amenable guest in the homes of the would-be fosters. He came back to the shelter and was installed in one of the cages in the back cat-room with the wild, sick, injured and otherwise doomed felines until he was in good enough shape to be put on display in the adoption room. In spite of his bad fostering experience, the staff needed to think that someone would want him—someone other than any of them.

Chester learned to open his cage in less than two days. The latch consisted of a metal rod that swung around and dropped into a slot on the cage door. The cat had to reach around with his paw, lift the metal piece and push the cage open while he held the piece up far enough to clear the slot, a difficult feat that no other cat—or dog—had mastered. There was a hole in the latch mechanism made for a padlock, but padlocks were generally used only for quarantined or dangerous animals. Chester became an exception.

In the daytime, Chester's cage stayed padlocked, but as often as they could get away with it, the officers on the evening and night shifts let him roam around the front office. At first, they tried to discourage him from settling in the outgoing mail tray, but eventually he won his place through perseverance.

Chester's coat grew less punk over time. He was a light orange tabby, almost salmon-colored. His coat was most like a Maine Coon's if he had to be attached to a breed of cat. His face remained that of an old prize fighter. His half-tail grew out to look something like a bottle brush. Although he was not a handsome cat, he had a certain presence.

Chester may have had annoying habits at his foster homes, but in the front office he was always a gentleman. His dislike of other cats did not disqualify him from being offered for adoption. When management decided it was time for him to go, he was supplied with the appropriate paperwork and placed in a prominent eye-level cage in the adoption room. No one adopted him in the requisite three days, so he stayed in his prime spot in the adoption room for more than two weeks. People appreciated his story, but he had flunked out of two foster homes—full disclosure. He was passed over in favor of younger, prettier cats with fewer distinctions. No one in the shelter could consider allowing him to be euthanized, not even the shelter manager who insisted it was time for him to go.

After some weeks of ignoring the untenable situation with Chester, the obvious solution finally manifested itself. The shelter needed a cat of its own. Other shelters had mascots. Why not ours? Chester was officially proclaimed Shelter Cat, and everyone heaved a sigh of relief.

Chester had the job of Shelter Cat for almost two years. He had been official for only about two weeks when I made his acquaintance. I worked in close proximity with him and he and I became close friends. Sometimes I talked to him when no one was around. His listening skills were as polished as any good dog's. My work days were not always filled with the most pleasant events. He always listened carefully, nodded wisely and rumbled soothingly. He was a fine counselor.

A reporter came in one day to write an article about Chester, whose story had spread. The local newspaper featured the story, complete with a picture of the cat in his favorite place as the "out-going male." Fame was to be his downfall. People began coming in just to see the famous shelter cat. Children wanted to hold him. He was not a cat who liked to be held. Some people asked to adopt him, but we were too attached to let him go. He had an important job that only he could do.

When Chester's celebrity made him into an object of public interest, we moved his tray behind the counter. During the busiest shelter hours, he spent his time in his padlocked cage for his own safety, but he still had a substantial amount of free time. He would never have left the shelter voluntarily. After more than a year and a half, he'd had plenty of opportunity to slip out the door, but he loved his home. We all like to think he loved us. When he disappeared one busy day, we had no doubt that he was taken away by some wretched human.

We did see him again. A little more than six weeks after his disappearance, he made his way back to the shelter. He must have traveled a long distance to get back home. Again, he was skinny. He was sick. He was dirty and matted. The vet said he was in total kidney failure this time, and it was time for us to let him go. The shelter staff mourned him. Animal lovers from all over brought and sent cards and flowers and toys in remembrance. Eventually his celebrity faded, but we missed him for a long, long time. We who had worked with him remembered him as cat of excellent character. I felt privileged to have known him and to have learned from him—things about tenacity and courage and perseverance and more.

Shortly after he left, we made the move to the new shelter building, and within a few weeks of the move, I was promoted to field officer. A small picture of Chester stayed in an unobtrusive place in the new office. We wanted to remember him, but we didn't want anyone asking questions about the cat in the outgoing mail tray. He was ours to remember. He was ours and he was not replaceable.

CHAPTER 4

DOGS AS FAMILY

Years ago, I liked to tell people that wolves raised me. The idea felt good, made me laugh and comforted me somewhat. The story was satisfying, but it wasn't true, not even as the obvious metaphor. My parents were not wolves. They were nice people, but they never gave that unconditional love and acceptance that wolves and dogs give their pups, and I couldn't talk to them about anything important (to me). They were mostly "children-should-be-seen-but-not-heard" people, like many other parents in that way. Mom noticed dirt on my hands and dog-hair on my clothes, but she was never interested in how it got there, or why. "Put that nasty shirt in the wash. You can't wear something like that to the dinner table."

I was a compliant child. "Ok, Mom."

Or the other thing she said a lot, "Put that dog outside."

I had a little pushback in me. "But, Mom!"

"Not another word. No. Outside."

We didn't have long conversations. Mom wasn't big on life tutorials or long-winded advice. She had enough trouble coping with her own busy life. Her mother wasn't big on tutorials either. Like me, I believe that Mom didn't receive enough early preparation for real life either. Few people do actually. We weren't that unusual.

I saved my long conversations for the animals, both living and stuffed. They weren't into tutorials or advice either, but they listened to every word I said, even if I didn't say it out loud. Dogs (the live ones) teach by example. They are teaching dog-skills, of course. Those are limited, but useful. My young, inexperienced parents did what they knew how to do. I missed many subtleties and some useful life-hacks learned at an early age by some others of my species. My self-esteem package came mostly second-hand, in pieces gathered from school, friends, teachers—dogs. Parts were missing.

Our family was small. Besides my two brothers and my parents, I had one aunt and uncle—my father's sister and her husband who lived in Singapore and then in England. They had some curb appeal: I very much liked the fact that Uncle James was a major in the Royal Army and had at one time been one of the stone-faced guards with the tall, fuzzy hats at Windsor Castle. Aunt Betty never had children. Her first husband was in the House of Lords, so she was a "Lady" until she divorced him because he beat her. Then she married Major James Selby Southworth. She and he were totally devoted to one another according to my mother. Every Christmas Aunt Betty and Uncle James sent us all silk pajamas. That was their entire contribution to our family life as far as I knew.

My mother was an only child. My brothers and I had no first cousins. Our maternal grandparents, Nanny and Grampy, were sweet, quiet people who usually lived nearby. Grandma Tilde, my father's mother, lived close to us for a while, but I don't think she thought of me as a real granddaughter, since my father had adopted me when I was two. All good people, my relatives, but they didn't have that simple-but-not-easy ability to give the nurture, support and direction that most mama wolves and dogs seem to be genetically hard-wired to provide to their pups. Some humans pass the art of raising children on to their offspring, along with loads of advice about how to get along in the world. Some don't. My parents were some that didn't. Luckily, I never wanted children. Not knowing how to raise them has never been a problem.

Growing up with a minimum of nurturing, active support or direction has consequences—good and not-so-good. One of my favorite consequences is that I learned to think for myself without a thick overlay of religion or strong opinions forced on me. Confidence in my own conclusions took a long time, but I reached a satisfactory place in relation to the world with less of a struggle than did some of my heavily-parented peers.

I give plenty of credit and gratitude for my satisfactory place to the descendants of wolves and a sprinkling of other species that have been important as members of my extended family—as friends, teachers and as potent good medicine. I would not have become me without them.

From dogs I learned that life can best be navigated with kindness, enthusiasm, good listening skills, sniffing out intentions, observing moods, and behaving well, except when misbehaving seems unavoidable. Dogs (and occasionally other animals) became essential medicine early in my life and have tended to show up serially as needed. For example, before we had a family dog, my day-care babysitter's cocker spaniel, Penny, did what she could to cheer me, although the babysitter's son Eric was a mean little bully.

Penny was a face-licker, loving everyone equally, even Eric. She may have taught me something about tolerance, since she saw the good in Eric-the-bully that was invisible to me. He was a year older than me, four and five to my three and four, during the year I spent my days at his house. Penny always made us laugh together. Eric was so much nicer when she was around. He had a rubber knife that he said would kill me if he decided to use it. I had some doubts about that rubber knife, but I couldn't take any chances with my life. I did whatever he wanted me to. We went into Tony's field, a cow field behind a barbed wire fence at the end of the block. Going in there was forbidden. When caught, we both got swatted with a ping pong paddle, and I knew I had been done a great injustice, but I couldn't say anything in my defense or Eric would have killed me—maybe. We played doctor, which I knew would get us in trouble if Eric's mother Dorothy found out. Playing doctor was interesting, but not much fun because I had to do everything he said. He was an unimaginative four-year-old. The experience was relatively benign. We never were caught at that game.

Eric's father, a "shell-shocked" ex-soldier, who worked as a gardener in a city-owned rose garden, sometimes took Penny into his den, where he stayed for hours. We were cautioned to stay out of Fred's way because, "He's in a bad mood. He won't tolerate any misbehaving from you two." Usually he was a kind, quiet man. He's the person who taught me to ride a bicycle. He had a missing middle finger which he tried to keep hidden, and he refused to say how he got it. "Accident, just an accident. Leave it be." He said the "Leave it be" with a chilling emphasis.

I missed Penny when Fred took her into his den and closed the door. Fred was home one or two days a week during my tenure there and he spent many hours of his time at home in his den, not always with Penny. Sometimes we would hear him knocking things around. Eric's mother Dorothy told us to "Never mind the noise. He's working something out. Go play outside." Or if the weather was bad, "Go play in the basement." Neither option boded well. I had to do what Eric wanted. Sometimes he pushed me or socked me in the arm if I wasn't doing something right, but I couldn't cry or make noise without risking worse. Eric was nicer when Penny was with us. My anxiety about the state of my small world increased ten-fold without her. Thinking back, I imagine the dog was working the magic that dogs do to help Fred cope with his shell shock. I remember Penny as a buffer between me and everything scary while I endured my day-care sentence at Eric's house. She was my first medicine dog.

CHAPTER 5

BOULOU

After Penny the cocker spaniel finished her work with me, our first family dog, Boulou came along. Boulou did not come to us because we went looking for a dog. My mother was a legal secretary, and her boss had a wealthy client who asked him to find someone to care for her poodle while she went to Europe for a few weeks. My mother couldn't very well say "no" to her boss, especially not in front of the chic, pushy client, so Boulou came to stay with us—temporarily. Weeks passed before the woman sent word that she had gotten married again and was staying in France. Her new husband had given her two small black poodles, which suited their lifestyle better than a big dog.

I heard Mom tell Dad what the lady said. "Honestly, that awful woman had the nerve to say, 'You may keep my Boulou,' as if she were bestowing the Pope's own blessing!" Mom wasn't pleased, but long before the "gifting," Boulou had become ours. The fact that she was an expensive pure-bred animal may have nudged my mother into appreciating her a little. Mom was a bit of a snob.

Every spring, Boulou received a poodle-ish haircut, shaved down to her pink skin, with tufts on her head, ears and tail. By late fall her coat had grown out so that she looked like a sheep. I was Mary and she was my little lamb for two Halloweens. She was my patient, huggable, smelly pillow, and the only one who understood the magnitude of my heartbreak when my father accidentally took my favorite stuffed animals to the dump. He and my mother were spring cleaning, and Dad accidently took the "keep" pile instead of the "throw-away pile" from my room. I can still get a lump in my throat over Kanga and Roo, and Blacky, my soft curly stuffed dog with floppy ears and a squeak. I cried for hours and hours, long after my father tried in vain to apologize and my mother became too impatient to deal with me. She sent me to my room. Boulou was there to listen, lick my tears away and offer comfort. I howled into her soft curls.

Boulou was always a willing playmate, too, not that I was lacking in human playmates. Our neighborhood was full of potential friends, and if I was too shy to approach any of them—and I was usually too shy—Boulou was happy to make introductions.

Our sweet poodle died quietly of old age in our garage when I was at school. We had moved from the house where her medicine was the most powerful when I was eight years old, because my brother Ken came into the family. We needed a bigger house. Boulou was getting old. She was still our good old dog, but my new baby brother took up most of the attention in the household. Boulou had to stay outside or in the garage all the time because of the baby. No amount of push-back or pleading from me could make Mom allow Boulou indoors.

Before our dog died, she slept most of every day for weeks, maybe months, out in the cold garage. At eight years old, I didn't think of her being out there after my first expressions of dismay went nowhere. I must have unconsciously prepared for her passing by pulling away from her. I stopped depending on her for the comfort and affection she had given so freely. That she may have needed some comforting at the end didn't occur to me. As with most dogs, she never asked for anything and she didn't complain. She was the family dog—an exceptionally fine example. I grieved hard when I heard the news of her passing, but the grief over her death passed more quickly than Boulou deserved, as I focused on my new brother and later on our next family dog.

CHAPTER 6

AN UNAVOIDABLE SIDE EFFECT

So many beautiful animals passed through the animal shelter, that wanting to take some of them home with me was unavoidable. My West Highland White Terrier, Tager, who had been with me since before I worked at Romar Kennels and then all through my five years in the Navy, was my faithful cheerleader and enthusiast. She welcomed all additions to the household.

By the time I began work at Seattle Animal Control, Tager was a senior citizen in dog years. We also lived with a large, dog-like tortoiseshell cat named Little Cat. Little Cat came to me as a tiny, 5-week old kitten that someone found in the neighborhood. At the time, my roommate had a full-grown Siamese cat. Somehow naming the little cat kept being put off until after the little cat had grown to twice the size of the Siamese. Little Cat remained Little Cat. That's who she was. The Cat part, though, became a misnomer, because Little Cat believed herself to be more dog than cat. Tager was her primary role model. She went on walks with us, trotting along beside Tager. She never walked on a leash because she didn't need one. No law said that cats had to be leashed. Fortunately, Little Cat was more street savvy than her role model. She handled being off leash with aplomb. Tager was not as street savvy as

Little Cat, nor did she always come when she was called. The cat was more dependable.

When I went to work as a kennel attendant, I had two licensed animals. The City Animal Code allowed each household three licensed animals. My third legal animal came home with me after I had been at my job for almost a month. She was an adorable little bob-tailed dog that looked like a miniature Welsh Corgi. She was about a quarter the size of one of the Queen's Corgis.

In the '80s, most of the dogs taken in by Animal Control were large dogs. Very few small dogs came into the shelter, unlike present-day shelters. Now most shelter dogs are small, but then the puppy-sized Corgi had to be housed in the puppy pen. She was much too small to be kenneled with big dogs and the kennel runs were overflowing with medium-sized and large dogs. Most small dogs that came in to the shelter were housed in the cat room and then, if not claimed, they were almost always adopted immediately. This little dog had a bad attitude that disqualified her for adoption. She barked uncontrollably at cats and she made the puppies in the puppy-pen scatter with a snap and a snarl. People who approached her faced a similar rebuff. She was going to be euthanized at the end of her three days if no one claimed her.

I knew her snarl was for show. She was scared and confused by the unfamiliar surroundings. She and I made friends after a short conversation in which treats were offered and accepted, but she remained thoroughly disgusted by the unruly puppies, and she continued to snarl at everyone who tried to approach her except me. I hoped that someone would come to claim her, but no one came. She was going to be put down and I couldn't let that happen. After my work-day was over, I smuggled her out to my car and brought her home. Tager thought she was okay. Little Cat thought she was perfectly all right. I named her Babs, and she stayed. She didn't get a license, however. I thought I might want to adopt some other animal through proper channels, and I only had one more legal license available.

I was a hypocrite when it came to the law about licensing animals. When my promotion to field officer eventually occurred, I would be charged with upholding all the city laws relating to domestic animals. Meanwhile, I let the licensing law drop by the wayside. My house and fenced yard had plenty of room for more than three animals. I couldn't save them all, but I intended to save as many as I could, within reason.

The third legally licensed animal came to live with us a couple of months after the addition of Babs. He was a four-month-old pit bull. Pit bulls were automatically euthanized. This one had been surrendered by his previous owner that day and was scheduled to be put down the next morning.

The little red-haired pup was rowdy and funny. During his first two years he tried my patience to the max and taught me a few things. Babs became "Nurse Babs" because she took care of the pit bull puppy and remained his attendant and protector for life. She chewed his whiskers and licked his face every chance she got and she nipped at his heels to convince him to move from where he was to wherever she thought he should be.

During my two years working in the kennel, I brought home many more animals. When I became a field officer, the practice continued. Finding homes for animals was an avocation. Most subsequent animals I found homes for, but my forever crew eventually topped out at five dogs and three cats. Besides numerous dogs and cats, the animals passing through my home included an Amazon parrot named Lucy, a white rabbit and two ferrets. Tager died at the age of fourteen in 1984, after living the exemplary life of a good dog.

CHAPTER 8

MRS. CALABASH

After my promotion to Animal Control Officer Two, I continued to save as many animals as I could from the final trip to the back room. My first rescue as a field officer I remember clearly. I recall standing on tiptoe to reach the back of a top-row metal cage, where a tiny, gray and white kitten hissed and spit, paws up, claws out, long hair fluffed, ready take on any enemy. She batted at my hand once or twice as I reached toward her, but she melted in surrender as my hand closed around her, as I knew she would. I lifted her out of the cage and kissed her on the nose before placing her in the deep pocket of my jacket.

After wiping down the cage, I removed the card clipped to the cage door and placed it on the stack of cards identifying the animals that had been euthanized earlier in the day. This kitty only died on paper. She was warm and safe in my pocket.

I had spent two years as a kennel attendant assisting the vet to euthanize hundreds of animals. Two years of doing that required dissociation, denial and suppression of daily heartbreak. Sometimes I was able to give a few animals longer than the allotted three days to try for adoption, but even then, not enough people came in to adopt the animals and more animals came in every day. More often than not, the dogs or cats with extra time met the same end as the ones that had only three days to be rescued. I understood that there was no reasonable alternative to killing the animals at the time. Few if any shelters anywhere could keep up with the prodigious numbers of unwanted animals—baskets and boxes of puppies and kittens, unwanted gifts, dogs that grew too large or unruly, inconvenient pets. Money and space were limited. The explosion of privately funded "no kill" kennels came later, after the pet-loving public finally woke up to what was happening— what is still happening—to animals in most government-funded shelters. Of course, many so-called "no-kill" shelters even today eventually give their old, sick or difficult animals to some other shelter where euthanasia is still common practice.

The vast majority of domesticated animals aren't able to survive on their own. Some of the animals brought to the city shelter where I worked were pets that had been abandoned in parks or wooded areas inside the city. Almost all of the abandoned strays were starving or sickly or worse, unless they were found within a few days of abandonment. Colonies of wild cats then, as now, were fed by well-meaning people, allowing the cats to produce offspring unprotected by vaccines. Sick, sticky-eyed kittens were and are still the result. If wild cats don't die of illness, they often serve as fast food for raccoons and coyotes.

The kitten that I removed from her cage was wild, born in a woodpile to a cat likely abandoned long before she gave birth to her kittens. An enterprising boy, whose driveway was adjacent to the woodpile, managed to capture one of the wild kittens under a box, but the boy was afraid to get the ferocious little beast out from under the box. His mother called Animal Control, asking for pick-up of a "wild cat," and I was the Animal Control Officer who answered the call, along with the officer who was training me. She stayed in the truck when we stopped at the house where we expected to find a contained wild cat.

I could see when I drove up to the house that there was a cat-sized cardboard box upside down on the driveway. Any self-respecting wild cat, even a sick one, would have flipped that flimsy box and scrambled away. The cat had to be: 1. Dead; 2. Near death; 3. Not wild at all; or 4. Very small.

I laid down flat on the driveway in order to lift the box just enough to illuminate the occupant with my flashlight. As it happened, this wild cat was number four, very small. She was a beautiful fluffy kitten not more than five or six weeks old. The kitten was not accustomed to the presence of humans. She was as wild as her mother taught her to be. Her mother had taught her how to behave when threatened. A hissing, spitting cat with claws out is a formidable creature, but the kitten was too cute to be convincing. I took her back to the shelter, but I could not force myself to allow her to be taken to the back room when her turn came to meet the needle, so I pocketed her and took her home. I called her Little Mrs. Calabash, because she spent most of her time in hiding.

Mrs. Calabash was aptly named. She grew into a beautiful long-haired gray and white cat, but few people ever saw her. Some of my friends thought she was imaginary. All her life she maintained her suspicious nature and avoided all humans except me. In her early years, she lived primarily in the basement of my house, among the black furnace vents that crisscrossed the ceiling. "Mrs. Calabash, come out, come out wherever you are." When I called her, she sometimes peeked out from behind whatever vent she was hiding behind, allowing certain privileged people to verify her existence. If I sat down, she would come sit on my lap and purr contentedly, allowing me to pet her, but she wanted nothing to do with me while I was standing up.

Mrs. Calabash was not difficult to put into a crate for transport to the vet when she needed shots. She liked dark, enclosed spaces. She tolerated being handled by the veterinarian, but she wouldn't talk to me for three or four days after she came home from a visit to the vet. She stayed with me for 18 years, through three moves, co-existing with a menagerie of dogs and cats. In her last years, she fell in love with a black cat I inherited from a friend. She and Becket did everything together. They were both exceptionally beautiful cats, and seeing them together was like watching living art.

Every once in a while, I was able to make a happy ending for one of the strays from the animal shelter. Happy endings made it possible for me to keep doing the job that I loved.

CHAPTER 8

A SINGULAR PIT BULL

Pit bulls are controversial for good reason, and owning one is not a chance I would take again, but one pit bull gave me more entertainment, love and fun than any other dog who came to live with me. A few of the animals I brought home stayed with me until death did us part. Robert Reddog was one who stayed. He was a dog whose habits as a young dog would have made him incompatible with most people, but I fell in love with him at first sight and stayed that way through mayhem, destruction, embarrassment and finally perfection.

When I came to work one day, while working as an Animal Control field officer, one of the kennel attendants grabbed me by the arm as I walked in the door. "You have to see this. Come on." He led me into the kennel area. In the second kennel run on the right was a four-month-old red pit bull puppy with a red bandana tied around his neck. As a pit bull, he was destined for immediate death. The shelter had a firm policy that no pit bulls were to be adopted out under any circumstances. Lloyd, the soon-to-be-retired kennel attendant whispered, "I checked him in as a boxer. If you want him, we better get the paperwork done now. I'm off shift and I'll take him home. You can pick him up after work."

"Oh, Lloyd, he's gorgeous! What a face! But I already

have two dogs, two cats and a foster dog with puppies. Why don't you adopt him?"

"My wife would kill me. And we're going to travel when I retire, after our old collie dies. I can't take this little guy, but he seems just right for you."

Lloyd knew that I was not one for thinking things over. My impulse control when it came to certain animals was close to nil. "Okay. Get the paperwork ready while I change into my uniform. I'll be down in five minutes to finish filling it out."

"No need to hurry. I filled it all out. Just come get him after you're off shift. You know where we live."

And so, handsome little Robert Reddog came to live with me and my menagerie. The golden retriever I had taken home a couple of weeks earlier decided to make Robert a sibling to her five-week-old puppies. Goldy the golden was a great mother, but her six black puppies were in bad shape when I picked them up. She and the pups had been found in a crawl space under a house. No one knew where she came from. Two of the puppies were close to death. I took all of them to my vet, Phyllis, and bypassed the shelter altogether.

Phyllis said she would look the dogs over and see what could be done. When I came back the next day, she had euthanized the two sickest puppies and had put the rest on antibiotics. I took them home to foster. Goldy was a beautiful young dog. She would be easy to place. Two of her puppies became blind from the infection in their eyes. I thought (wrongly) that they might be a problem. A friend knew a couple who had owned two blind Labradors for years. When their dogs died, they weren't planning on replacing them, but when the couple heard about Goldy's blind puppies, they couldn't help themselves. They came to see them. They regaled me with wonderful stories about the Labradors, and they took the blind puppies home with them. The other two pups were easy to place.

Goldy taught Robert better dog manners than I could have taught him. She flattened him with a growl when he got too rowdy. He learned to play gently with his comparatively tiny siblings, and he learned to respect the cats.

In the following months, Robert stayed home with my other dogs and the roommate who rented my two basement rooms. My roommate enjoyed the animals. She knew what she was getting into when she came to live in my house with her cat. She was almost always home when I wasn't. Robert didn't feel lonely.

When the roommate moved out, Robert was about a year old. He was madly energetic, maniacally happy about everything and enormously strong, but he had given me only one truly alarming pit bully episode. When he was around six months old, I had taken him with me to the store on a rainy day and had left him alone in my 1969 Volvo sedan for about ten minutes. When I came back to the car, both of the front seats, most of the back seat and the side panels in the doors were shredded, leaving stuffing and bits of red fabric all over. Robert definitely had the pit bull jaws of steel, and, apparently, he also had separation anxiety. For a while, I put him in a crate or left him with friends when I was away from the house. I never left him upstairs alone. He behaved like any ordinary, energetic, light-hearted, reckless, poorly-trained dog.

One sunny spring day I thought Robert would be fine if I left him with my other two dogs in the basement for a few hours, out of his crate. I hated having to crate him on such a beautiful day. Goldy and her pups had found their homes weeks before this happened. When I came home, Robert had pulled a box spring and mattress from the downstairs bedroom through two other rooms to the doggy door. He tore both mattress and box-spring apart and carried most of the pieces out to the yard. Then he dragged the bed-frame to the door, but he was unable to take it apart. I'm sure he tried. He had some serious separation anxiety. The other two dogs weren't exciting enough company for him. They were pretending they didn't know him when I found the carnage.

After that adventure, I tried to keep Robert's anxiety in mind and make appropriate arrangements for him whenever I left the house, but there were a couple of times I failed in adequately acknowledging his condition. Once he tore apart two feather pillows. I picked up stray feathers in the basement for many months.

Another time, Robert dug under the fence and all four of my dogs got out while I was at work. A German Shorthair pointer had come to live with us by that time. Maggie was a very responsible dog. She stayed on the covered front porch while the other three dogs were picked up by Animal Control. A neighbor had called about the loose dogs. My fellow-officer, Mitch, said over the radio, "Picked up three strays, including a nice red boxer-mix at the corner of 6th Ave NE and NE Third. They have ID, so I'll see if I can find the owner." Everyone understood that message meant my dogs. I never lived that one down.

Robert was a wussy pit bull. I was lucky in that respect, because very few pit bulls are voluntarily submissive. He was attacked by a German Shepherd once while we were walking on a beach. Robert was on a long leash. The Shepherd ran free. The fight lasted all of five seconds before Robert was on his back. The Shepherd picked up the ball he had been carrying and trotted away, leaving Robert slightly embarrassed but uninjured. Ordinarily the story doesn't end that way when a pit bull is involved in a fight. Robert was an anomaly.

When he was just over two years old, Robert settled into becoming a practically perfect dog. I became a volunteer at a prison program where the inmates trained dogs, and Robert was used as a guinea pig for training the inmates to train service dogs. He learned to obey the usual obedience commands—heel, come, sit, down, stay—and he learned several other things. He could hold a biscuit on his nose and on command he would toss it up and catch it. He would play dead if someone pointed a finger and said "bang." He rolled over—and over and over and over. He jumped through hoops and over barriers and he would fetch anything—car keys, the phone, a pen, a dime....

Robert was not only a handsome dog with a great sense of humor, he also gave me more stories, more trouble and more laughs than any of my other pets. He taught me a few things, like how to install car seats from a salvage yard and how to really dog-proof a fence. He taught me that I am one of those people who thinks dogs are worth it, no matter what "it" is.

CHAPTER 9

ENGLISH SETTERS AGAINST ANGST

In line with my wolf-dog fantasy, my after-school job in high school involved a pack of dogs. I groomed English Setters, twelve show dogs belonging to Anne, a friend of my mother's. Besides working as a court reporter, she bred and showed her English Setters. She and her husband owned a small property outside of town, on the road to Virginia City, with a small house for a caretaker, a dozen dog kennels and everything else a show dog needed. The property was called "Rocky Nevada Kennels." Joe, the caretaker, lived there and looked after the dogs and the property. In town, Anne had a larger house that was a short bus ride from my high school. She rotated three or four of her dogs from the kennels to the house in town every week. After school I spent time grooming the dogs, allowing their patience and affection and goofy enthusiasm to help mellow high school angst and turbulence.

High school was high drama for me, as it was for most of my friends. High school is almost always high drama, but my friends were a particularly unusual and dramatic group at Reno High School in the 1960s—adolescence intensified by a high percentage of alternate lifestyles and creative dysfunction. Reno was still called "The Divorce Capital of the World" in the '60s, although divorce laws were changing around the country. "The Biggest Little City in the World," with its gambling industry, attracted an interesting cross-section of non-standard people, some of whose children were my best friends. Oddly (to me) I was voted "Most Unusual" at my high-school graduation, which I took as an honor. My friend Roger was voted "Most Unusual" of the opposite gender. He wrote comic books about a character called "Super Scheenie" with my prom date, Mario, one of few Jewish students at Reno High. Mario came from Italy, spoke many languages and lived by himself. Roger and I thought he was, without doubt, the most unusual student at Reno High, but the votes favored me and Roger. Being officially Most Unusual just made us feel more like consecrated Renoites, typical examples of our kind. We liked each other. Being partners under the Most Unusual banner was an honor.

My circle of friends was a little nerdy, a little fringy, a little crazy, mostly middle-class white kids with lots of curiosity and a minimum of parental guidance. We were all reasonably good students, but probably not as good as we could have been with a little more effort—but real life was so much more thrilling, surprising, and full of passion than schoolwork.

My best friend, Kaley, had two closeted mothers. She was arrow straight, which was more than a little disappointing, since I had a crush on her and was beginning to have arguments and discussions with myself about being a lesbian. She sympathized but couldn't empathize. My ersatz boyfriend Chris was also gay. He lived with his father because his mother had been committed to a mental institution. We were all dealing with our high school experience with the usual emotion and volatility of high school kids, on top of some additional special circumstances.

One of the most significant special circumstances from my life involved meeting a brother I hadn't known existed. We met in a parking lot after a football game. The parking lot near the football field consisted of gravel and dirt with no markings to delineate individual spaces. Parking there was based on who got there first and who decided to keep the lines of cars in lines. More often than not, people parked as a statement of independence from the mainstream, which made exiting the lot at the end of the game a long, irritating, dusty, noisy event. Sometimes this big guy named John directed traffic. He was 6 feet 7 inches tall and weighed over 300 pounds, so he was easy to see. He made getting out of the lot a more orderly process.

John didn't go to our school. He was almost twenty-one. He could buy beer without being carded. I don't know if he ever actually graduated from high school. Book-learning definitely wasn't his thing, but he excelled in making friends. He was good looking, always smiling and always interested in whoever he was talking to. He was also guileless. He loved football but had never played the game in school, and he loved coming to the high school games. The football team liked him. He was their good luck charm, or maybe a kind of mascot. Everybody recognized Big John Bolander. I had never spoken to him, but I knew who he was. Sometimes I wondered if he might be a distant cousin.

My biological father's last name was Bolander. It isn't a common name, but it isn't uncommon, either. After a football game to which I was allowed to drive my mother's car, my friend Kaley and I were stopped in the knot of traffic trying to exit the parking lot. Traffic wasn't moving. John came over to my car to say hi.

I rolled down my window. He asked how we were and said something about "you pretty young ladies." Being singled out by John was a special distinction. His smile was full of light and besides being darkly handsome, he was a sweet man, so sweet it almost made me want to cry after I got to know him better. At some point in our first conversation I told him that my last name had been the same as his for the first two years of my life. "Really? Who's your father?"

"Ummm, his name is Jim. I don't remember him at all. I think he's a private detective in Los Angeles or someplace." I was a little taken aback by the question, which seemed a little too personal.

John stepped back from the car, raised his hands and boomed, "You're my sister!" just as the traffic started to move again.

Kaley couldn't believe he said what he said. "What did he say? Does he think you're his sister because you had the same last name once-upon-a-time?"

"I think he meant that Jim Bolander is his father, too."

We were about to begin moving toward the exit. John hurriedly wrote his number on a scrap of paper that he handed through the window. "Call me!"

He was my half-brother. My mother had told me early on that I had a biological father different from my real father, who had adopted me when I was two, but she didn't mention that Jim Bolander, my bio-dad, had another child. John's mother was a Paiute from the reservation north of Reno. When she was twenty-one, she married Jim, who was sixteen, so that their baby wouldn't be stigmatized by being a bastard. Being a bastard was a black mark then. So Jim did the right thing and then went off to join the Navy. He and John's mother divorced while John was still a baby. I had this giant older brother all of a sudden—as if high school wasn't already full to the brim.

Along with a new branch to my social life, John brought questions about family and more anxiety, misery and intrigue to my emotional life. Kaley and I and several of my other friends spent time with him. We—mostly they--enjoyed the fact that he was generous with everything he had, including booze. I didn't like to drink, although I did drink a little sometimes, to fit in, but alcohol inevitably made me anxious. It wasn't in the least bit happy-making, no matter how much I wanted it to be.

John had a huge crush on Kaley (too). She said at some point that she felt bad for leading him on. I don't think she did that, but I remember that too often when I was nice to a boy he seemed to think I was flirting. I wasn't. I was just being friendly. Sometimes being friendly got me into trouble. I had a couple of marriage proposals that came as a big surprise from friends who stopped being friends after my guilty, but definite NO. More than once boys assumed I was willing to go farther than I was willing to go.

Anyway, John had a better chance with Kaley than I did, even though I knew he had no chance at all. He probably didn't figure that out for a long time. She was just being friendly. She may have felt bad for "leading him on." I felt bad for a whole host of other reasons. Kaley couldn't help breaking my heart, and she was helpless to stop doing it because she was—as most typical teenage girls are—completely boy crazy. Still, we were the closest of friends, passing notes and sharing experiences non-stop as life frantically exploded all around us.

I was still trying to cope with the unwanted realization that I was a lesbian. Sometimes I tried to play along with the pack, losing my virginity to a blue-eyed boy named Jerry. He didn't go to our school. I never saw him again, but at least I crossed that hurdle. In the 60s it was a hurdle for some, made more popular by birth control and the changing social norms. Navigating hormones and feelings without a map made for some tricky challenges.

Though some of my male friends were gay, they were part of an entirely different culture/lifestyle than lesbians. My boyfriend Chris and I played at wanting to be straight, including having sex, which was physically fun and somewhat dangerous. We didn't think much about birth control. He and I both knew that having fun in bed didn't change either of us, but we had a little fantasy life going on, a little longing to be part of the many instead of part of the few. We played a version of Russian Roulette, but we managed to keep me from getting pregnant. We talked about little cottages with picket fences, but all the while Chris was swooning for love of (slightly sadistic) Richard, and I for love of Kaley.

Through Chris I had some gay male friends but I knew of no lesbians except Kaley's mothers, and they weren't owning up. Their closet was deep and dark. I needed all the dog-time I could get to stay afloat. My job with the setters was an enormous blessing. They had no opinions where no opinions were needed and they thought I was great exactly the way I was. They were sweet and uncomplicated, slow-moving, unself-conscious and soothing.

Grooming an English setter for show is a long, tedious

process, but I loved it. Focusing on the dogs was a meditation. The hair on their backs must be plucked, not shaved. Their ears needed to be shaped just so. The feathers (long hair) on their tails and lower bodies required constant brushing, shaping and de-matting. The dogs visibly appreciated the attention. They were beautiful, mellow and malleable. I loved that the brown spots on their sleek white coats made the hair that gathered on the dog brush a pretty salmon color. My after-school-job had dream-job potential, including a generous wage for the time, but after the first year, it began to include too much gritty real-life activity to hit the mark dead center.

After school, I took the bus or drove my mother's car to Anne's house, three or four times a week and spent two hours or more working on the dogs. At first, my relationship with my employer—a tiny, skinny, wrinkled little woman who looked older than her late fifties—was cordial but strictly employer to employee. I usually did my work in an enclosed patio area in the back of the house. If Anne had specific instructions, she wrote them down. She sat near the house reading, always with an iced drink on the table next to her and dogs at her feet. In warmer weather, her matchstick legs emerged from a pair of black shorts, even though she constantly complained about the cold, no matter the season or the temperature.

After I had worked for Anne for several weeks, she gradually became more talkative, and began telling me about the dogs and their histories. She moved her chair closer to the work-table, and over a period of another several weeks we became friendly as I brushed and trimmed Balloo or Dolly or whoever was on the table that week. They all smelled like a meadow of flowers. They were bathed at the kennel every three or four months, or before a show.

Balloo became a rag doll on the table, allowing me to move him into any position and holding absolutely still until I moved him again. He felt boneless, like a cat. Dolly was ticklish. She tensed up if I got too close to the ticklish place on her belly, and her back leg started to vibrate. Some of the other dogs had the same common tickle-response, but Dolly was apologetic about it, overly apologetic. Her exaggerated expressions would have made her famous on YouTube if she were alive today.

Anne asked a little about school, about my activities, but she would not talk about herself except in relation to the dogs. She told me about one of her first dogs, still and forever her favorite, although the dog was long dead. I listened to the entire history of Toni, aka Hi-Antonia of Rocky Nevada—every show, every ribbon, every trophy, every wonderful thing the dog had ever done, her perfect head, her perfect tail-set. Toni started Anne's obsession with setters. She had favorite dogs among the ones I knew, but none of them matched long-departed Toni.

Most of the setters I knew were related to Toni. Dolly was a granddaughter and had more than her share of cups and ribbons. In terms of the breed standard, Dolly was as practically perfect as her grandmother, but I couldn't distinguish perfect setters from imperfect setters. They all looked regal and beautiful, like they should be in an 18th century painting, lounging in a field on a British estate. I never could have been a dog show judge. How could anyone dissect the gorgeousness of these creatures and make one better than all the others?

When I had worked for Anne for almost a year, she introduced me to Rocky Nevada Kennels. The man who took care of the house, a quiet, polite young Mexican man—Joe—picked us up in a Chevy Suburban. The three dogs that were returning to their kennel-home with him jumped into their crates behind the seats without coaxing. Joe secured the crate doors, made sure Anne and I were settled, and drove us south. He made a left turn off the highway onto a road that disappeared in the distance, curving up into the desert foothills toward Virginia City. The Kennels were a mile or two down the road, before it began its ascent into hills. The desert scrub on both sides of the road contained a few houses and randomly placed trailers.

The little house at Rocky Nevada Kennels was an anomaly in the downscale neighborhood. The property was a little island in the middle of sagebrush and tumbleweeds. Its salmon-pink color was close to the color of the liver and white setters' hair mixed together in a palette. The pristine kennels in back were built of cinder blocks painted white with chain link runs, two sets of six kennel-runs facing each other across a grass exercise yard. The entire back yard of the house was enclosed by a six-foot cinderblock wall, also painted white. Across the back wall, a wooden building with four evenly spaced doors held all the equipment necessary to care for the dogs—for feeding, bathing, transport, and whatever else the dogs might need.

Joe lived in the house and kept it and the dogs in immaculate condition. He bathed the dogs and brushed them but he didn't groom them. The house had little furniture. Everything in it was spotless. In the living room, one wall was taken up by a huge glass case displaying trophies, silver platters, silver bowls, plaques, ribbons and certificates won by Anne's dogs. Every big win was captured in a photo on a plaque, showing the dog, the judge and the dog's handler. Anne didn't handle her own dogs in the show ring.

Hi-Antonia of Rocky Nevada had her own smaller

case on an adjoining wall with dozens of items made of silver, several plaques with pictures and layers of ribbons, mostly blue ones. Besides the photos from shows, other pictures showed Toni with puppies, Toni with Anne and Anne's husband Ray, and Toni with the man who had been the dogs' handler since the beginning of Rocky Nevada Kennels. Bud, the handler, had been both friend and employee for more than twenty years.

I had never known anyone so devoted to or obsessed with dogs and dog shows, and all the trimmings, as Anne. Show dogs require a lot of time, attention and equipment. I wasn't drawn to the dog show world, but I understood the need to have dogs, the reasons to care for dogs, the restorative value of dogs. Anne stood in front of Toni's display case with tears in her eyes. I was out of my comfort zone. Joe brought me a coke. He motioned toward the kitchen, indicating I could sit at the table while he loaded up the dogs that were going to stay in town for the week. Anne took some time with her memories.

The hair collected from brushing the dogs went into paper bags, stacked and saved in a closet. The hair from the one black and white setter in the group went into its own separate bag. Anne took the bags into the house as I filled them up. She told me she was keeping the hair for a project, but at first, she wouldn't tell me any specifics about the project. During our trip to the Kennels, she finally explained. She told me that the dogs had saved her life and were her life—no details, just that. She had spent time thinking about how she could honor them and express their importance to her, and she came up with the idea of making a coat from the setters' hair.

The coat project had been in process for three or four years. When she had a certain number of full bags, she sent them off to someone who spun the hair into wool and mailed back pinkish skeins. Anne had been collecting skeins to have them knit into a long coat that she had designed. The stash of setter wool was in a secure cupboard, waiting to be processed into the final product. With a few more skeins, she would be ready to send the design and the wool to a knitter who would transform the wool into her long-awaited fabulous coat.

Anne had an impressive background. I learned a little from my mother, who told me Anne was the only child of a prominent politician in Nevada. Her mother had died when she was young. She was the youngest person to ever graduate from the University of Nevada at the age of 17. She was a music teacher for a few years, and she acquired a law degree, but she never practiced law. Instead she worked as a court reporter for the same judge for whom my mother worked as a legal secretary.

Mom cautioned me to never let Anne drive me anywhere—because she was "not well," and she was a terrible driver. I didn't know what "not well" meant, and my mother didn't elaborate. Anne had a slight tremor; she was also extremely thin. I thought she probably had some kind of chronic disease but didn't speculate too much. I knew to keep my questions to a minimum. Mom didn't like sharing other peoples' personal information any more than she shared her own. I probably learned more about Anne from her than she intended to tell me.

During my second year of grooming the setters, Anne asked me to accompany her to a dog show. The first show we went to was a specialty show, a show just for English Setters. It took place about 30 miles away, in Carson City.

I had my driver's license by that time, and I drove Anne's Range Rover with three of her dogs in crates in the back, along with all of their equipment. When we arrived at the show, a tall, thin man wearing tight black pants and a white turtleneck with a picture of an English Setter on the front met us in the parking area. Anne introduced me to Bud, her long-time dog handler. I recognized him from the pictures in the glass case at the Kennels, but he was dressed and coifed a little more formally in the pictures. When I met him, his unnatural shade of thick auburn hair was done in a half-Elvis, half-rooster style that would have made me laugh out loud if I had been less polite. Bud appeared to be several years younger than Anne, dramatic and effeminate, which I thought infinitely interesting. He took me and the setters in hand as my employer disappeared into a trailer that belonged to some old friends, fellow setter-people. I learned from Bud that Anne was busy getting "sloshed" in that trailer with her "alky" friends. He was astonished to find out that I hadn't noticed she was an alcoholic. The thought had never occurred to me.

Bud showed me tricks for getting the dogs to look their best in the show ring. He told me about some of the other breeders and their dogs. As we worked at last-minute fluffing and plucking and shaping, he filled me in on the rules of show and the important gossip about a few dog owners, breeders, handlers, judges—a brief introduction to back-stage politics. He also told me more about Anne's background. I listened to his every word, all the while hoping for an opening to let him know I was gay, too. The opportunity never arrived. He talked non-stop.

Bud told me Anne's mother had died of influenza when Anne was only ten years old. Her mother had been a violinist and Anne spent years training to be a concert violinist, besides being a wunderkind in a dozen different ways, collecting two master's degrees before she turned 20. "I met her at some party in the hazy days after the war. Believe it or not, she was a pretty girl. We all drank too much then and didn't think much about it. Drinking was the thing to do. She and I clicked when we started talking about dogs. I was new to the show circuit. She taught me most of what I know about showing these lovelies. (Here he kissed Dolly on her head). Back then we both drank ourselves silly regularly. I must have hauled her home, wrangled the dogs and tucked her in a hundred times before she married Ray. Seems like a long time ago. I suppose it was. Now the two of them stay home and drink, except when she comes to shows, and I'm twelve years sober. Seeing what she's become breaks my heart, but there's nothing to be done about it—you know—unless she wants to change and she doesn't want to."

"When did she stop playing the violin?" I forgot to bring up the gay thing.

"Oh, some time before I met her. The violin doesn't pair well with gin and tonic. Dogs aren't so demanding." He lifted Pogo onto the grooming table. "This boy isn't going to win, but he has the attitude of a winner. He's just a little old for the game, like me." He posed with one hand on his hip and made me laugh.

Anne's dogs didn't win anything at the Carson City show. She looked sober to me when she came out of the trailer. She groused a little about losing—the judge was "either blind or crooked"—but then she fell asleep in the car before Bud and I had everything loaded up. The dogs that we took to that show all had their fair share of ribbons already. They were getting too old to compete. When we arrived back at the house, I was on my own, unloading dogs and equipment.

I finally knew what my mother meant by saying Anne wasn't well. Her husband came out of the house while I was unloading and helped her out of the car. The two of them walked unsteadily into the house without saying a word to me—a day full of life-lessons brought to me through my association with dogs. I wondered how dogs had saved Anne's life. She felt she owed them, but obviously they didn't do anything to subdue her drinking.

The second and last dog show that I attended with Anne was at the Cow Palace in San Francisco. We went by train over the mountains. During the four-hour-plus trip, I spent most of my time in the baggage car with the setters. They were seasoned travelers. They napped the whole way, but I didn't want to leave them alone in the dank, dark baggage car. One of the porters pulled a heavy wooden bench from somewhere in the car. He set it up facing the dog crates. I sat there, talking to the dogs as they slept, listening to the train sounds. Anne spent the entire trip in the bar car.

This time we took the best show dogs, the ones that might still have a chance against younger competition, Dolly and Blue Boy. Blue Boy was the only one of Anne's setters that had a black and white coat. His hair outlined the pockets and decorated the lapels on the fabulous coat, which had come in the mail a few days before. At the San Francisco station I had to coordinate transport of the dogs and of my staggering drunk employer to the hotel, duties that were beyond my job description. She was undeniably drunk during most of the trip, and this time her condition was obvious.

The gorgeous full-length setter-hair coat was amazing. Taking it out of its box, I noticed how heavy it was, even though it was almost child-sized for Anne. The tight double knit was softer than cashmere. Anne said it was more expensive than the finest mink and worth every penny. She said that before she tried it on and found that it was too heavy for her to wear. Her frail little body couldn't carry the heavy coat more than a few steps, but we took it to San Francisco anyway. We didn't talk about it after the disaster of trying it on. I helped her lay it out on the second bed in her hotel room. She had booked a separate room for me and, to my surprise, allowed both dogs to spend the night in my room.

I spent too much time on that trip making sure Anne didn't hurt herself or throw up in public—not a reality I was used to. At home she seldom if ever showed evidence of drunkenness. The coat must have sent her over some edge.

Before the show I spent some time with Bud and the dogs, but there wasn't much for me to do while the dogs were in the ring. Watching the competition made me nervous, the same way beauty pageants made me nervous. What about the un-perfect dogs? What about the less-than-perfect girls? Why were these people so desperate for their animals to win? A tiny bit of feminist sensibility involving the injustice of beauty crept into my consciousness around that time, but my real feminist paradigm-shift happened after high school, and after the Summer of Love.

The dogs were all magnificent, every breed, winners and losers. Most of them were works of kinetic art. I wandered among them behind the scenes while Anne went off her with friends again, after telling me where we should meet when it was time to go back to the hotel. Dolly won a third-place ribbon, which we didn't discuss. Third place wasn't worth celebrating.

My job grooming setters ended within a few weeks of

the Cow Palace show. Anne went into the hospital where she stayed for a long time with liver problems. The hospital said she didn't want visitors. Mom sent flowers and added my name to the card. As far as I know, the setters never went to another show. Anne sent a short, shakily written message a few weeks into her hospital stay thanking me for my work and saying that she wouldn't be needing my help any more. My mother told me she had quit her court reporting job because of her failing health. She severed communications with her friends at the courthouse. I never heard from her again.

Several years later, my mother sent me her obituary. Anne died in a nursing home at the age of sixty-five. The obituary said she left three beloved English setters, and her husband Ray. No other relatives were mentioned. I had been away from home for a few years by that time.

Anne's dogs were vital medicine for me, even if some of the medicine was bitter. Anne's life provided an up-close view of one kind of tragedy—the inability to inhabit the extraordinary gifts she was given because of an addiction. I don't know how her dogs saved her, but she said they did somehow. Dogs can teach and entertain, save and comfort, love without judgement, but they can't fix everything.

CHAPTER 10

MICHAEL AND THE CANNONS

When I first went to work at Animal Control, the shelter was a converted warehouse located at the foot of Queen Anne hill, about a mile south of the future shelter. When the temporary shelter passed its first year of operation, we gave up believing the projections that the city created every few months for completion of the new building. Each projection pushed the time farther out—6 months, 8 months, a year, 14 months, 15 months.... We were able to see how the construction was progressing by driving by the hole in the ground that was to be our modern new building, two stories complete with modern design and a spay/neuter clinic. A little work happened periodically, but at the rate they were building, we figured we would be long dead by the time the new shelter emerged from the hole in the ground.

The converted warehouse didn't have the most efficient setup for kennels, nor did it facilitate the best working conditions, but it had one notable perk. On the Fourth of July, the shelter's second story and its parking lot provided a near-perfect view of the fireworks over Elliot Bay. Not only would we be able to see the display overhead, the barge with the cannons that launched the fireworks was in the water near enough so that the launches could be seen, heard and felt—"the total experience," according to the people who had seen the event from the original shelter. The old shelter, which no longer existed, had been directly across the street from the temporary location. The old shelter had been directly adjacent to Elliot Bay—not ideal for the dogs and cats, but great for the staff's view of the fireworks. Shelter staff did their best to keep the animals from hurting themselves or one another, but inevitably there were minor casualties among the terrified animals.

At the new temporary location, we were only about 400 feet away from where the old shelter had stood. The fireworks barge was still close enough to provide "the total experience." We were told that the cinderblock construction of the warehouse building would provide a little more insulation from the noise than the old wooden structure. "A little more" may have been slightly better, but we knew it was far from enough.

I volunteered to work the night shift on July 4, 1981. I worked the same hours as one of the two late-shift field officers. We would be working a ten-hour shift. Mine started at 7:00 pm, at the same time as my friend Michael, a field officer, came on duty. The other field officer came on shift in the late afternoon and was already out answering calls. I was a relatively new employee, still a kennel attendant. Kennel attendants didn't ordinarily work night shifts, except on July Fourth. On most other nights the late shift was slow and easy about 50% of the time, except when the police department called for assistance with some kind of emergency—barking dog, injured stray, or a dog needing to be impounded because of some other police-related incident. Other animal emergencies happened late at night, but only a few were remarkable. The Fourth of July had the potential to be remarkable with numerous police calls regarding animals.

Dozens of emergencies happened because of freaked-out animals. Once a call came in to look for a large dog that had hurled itself through a plate glass window. The dog was eventually located seven miles away from its home, limping along on adrenaline and a dislocated hip. The police often picked up strays and dropped them at the shelter on the night of July Fourth because so many panicked animals were on the streets. AC field officers couldn't handle all the calls. One of my tasks was to check in the drop-offs.

I volunteered to work the Fourth for the double-time pay and for the chance to watch the fireworks from one of the best vantage points in the city. I was prepared for a busy night, but hoped it would allow me time to watch some of the fireworks display. The Space Needle had its own spectacle going on while colored lights exploded in the air above in time to music piped out over the Bay. At the beginning of my shift, I felt excited and fortunate to be able to be there for the show. Michael came into the shelter around 9:00 pm to unload his truck and to wait for some of the police emergencies that would start coming in when the fireworks began. He also helped me do what we could for the animals to prepare them for the coming event.

The dogs in the shelter couldn't be shielded from the massive noise of the cannons. We could only try to make sure none of them hurt themselves or each other during the explosions. Some of the dogs that seemed to be more likely to be affected by the fireworks were moved to banks of portable cages that we rolled into the adoption room, located between the front office and the kennels. Being in a small enclosed space helped lessen anxiety in some of the more high-strung dogs. The cats were in individual cages in two rooms to the west of the adoption room.

They weren't likely to hurt themselves. We turned off the lights in the cat rooms and hoped for the best.

Michael was an ex-marine who had fought in Vietnam. He joined the Marines as more of a rebellion against his family than a burning need to serve. He said he didn't feel that he should sit safe at home while friends went off to risk their lives. His father was a doctor; his grandfather was a doctor, and Michael was supposed be a doctor, according to the unwritten family charter. He entered the University of Washington and could have kept his student deferment, but in the middle of his second year, he joined the Marines. Immediately after training, he went to Vietnam. He was soft-spoken, soft-hearted, intelligent, interesting and funny. We always had something to talk about and we enjoyed each other's company. He never talked about his experiences as a Marine.

We were sitting in the front office of the animal shelter, waiting for the fireworks to start. My job later that night was to act as dispatcher and to patrol the building and look in on the animals periodically when the radio calls slowed. At that time, the dog kennels were overcrowded, as usual, and held around a hundred dogs. The cat room cages contained about twenty cats and kittens and one ferret. The quarantine room behind the cat room held another dozen cats that were either sick or wild, destined for euthanasia. Until the early hours of the morning, besides looking in on the animals, the rest of my time was to be spent answering calls from the police dispatcher and relaying calls in order of importance to Michael and the other field officer. The police pitched in where they could. After midnight, things usually slowed down.

The Fourth of July and the day after were the busiest and most distressing days at the Animal Control Shelter. I didn't know how busy and distressing. All over the city frantic animals escaped confinement. Some of them were hurt—not always, but usually from being hit by cars. Crazed dogs sometimes damaged property. People who put their dogs in their cars, thinking the car a safe and secure place, sometimes came back to find the upholstery and interior in shreds. Normally docile animals bit people in their panic over the noise. Some people don't easily forgive those kinds of destructive behavior. An abundance of pets and strays were always surrendered to the shelter in the days directly after the Fourth, and the number of strays that were picked up by field officers increased by half.

Around 9:30 pm, the neighbors up the hill from the shelter started shooting off small fireworks. Michael stood up in the middle of our conversation and seemed to have a sudden change in mood. His face went pale. "Maybe this isn't a good idea," he said mostly to himself. I thought maybe he was feeling sick. We had been talking about fireworks and shows we remembered back to childhood. We were looking forward to going outside to watch at least part of the big show, which was supposed to start in a few minutes. I barely noticed the sounds of small fireworks from up the hill. Sparks were coming down into the parking lot outside. They were visible through the glass double doors.

When the first of the big cannons went off, Michael ran out the front door into the parking lot. I followed him. He yelled, "Get down! Get down! Take cover!" Before I caught up with him, he was down on the ground rolling under a car, still yelling. I was stunned and confused. Cannons began going off at more or less regular intervals, in sync with the blaring music. The dense crowd across the street, barely visible in the dark, was saying, "Oooo, and Ahhh." The blasts were deafening, but I didn't really notice them. I was frozen in place, waiting for Michael to come back to himself, hoping that he would come back. I hadn't the slightest idea what was going on, but I knew something was horribly wrong with my friend. I had never heard of PTSD back then, and I thought shell-shock was something that happened more immediately after a traumatic experience in a war, not years later.

My grandfather was a British soldier, a rifleman, discharged from WWI with a serious leg injury and "shell-shock," according to his discharge paper, which I found online long after he died. I imagined he was all better—except for his slight limp—by the time I knew him. Now I wonder. He never spoke about himself, and if pressed, he made up stories about his past. His version of the war had nothing to do with the reality. He said he was a bombardier, flying above the fray. He lied about his brother Alec. Alec died at the Battle of the Somme, the same battle in which my grandfather was injured. My grandfather said only that Alec died young in an accident. We didn't find out about the truths of his past until after his death, but I came to believe that his lies were evidence that the Battle of the Somme stayed with him long after his discharge from the Royal Infantry. Michael was discharged from the Marines in 1976, five years before the fireworks episode.

After a few minutes of panic, Michael rolled out from under the car and brushed himself off. His face was dripping with sweat, or maybe tears. I could see he was feeling flustered and embarrassed. I turned around and went back into the shelter. He followed after a few minutes.

All he said as he passed my desk was, "Joke's over. I'll check on the dogs. You can keep watching if you want."

The cannons were still going off and the crowd making appreciative noises but I didn't care. Maybe Michael went into the kennels to soak up some dog medicine, to lower his blood pressure, to hug a sympathetic, non-judgmental warm body. I hoped so. I would have done just that right then, if he hadn't sought the company of the dogs first. Maybe he just went in there to get away from me, the witness to his incongruous behavior.

Radio calls began coming in. In less than 10 minutes I had taken three calls that needed to be handled as soon as possible. I was mechanically doing triage on the incoming calls, separating emergencies from things that could wait, trying to calm people who were freaking out about their animals or someone else's animals while writing down the calls on cards. Some calls I radioed to the officer already in the field. I had three call-cards in my hand when Michael emerged from the kennel. The explosions continued. They lasted for only twenty minutes, but it seemed longer. Firecrackers, sounding like gunshots in the distance, continued to go off as Michael popped through the door of the adoption room heading for his truck in the parking lot. As he passed me, he grabbed the three cards from my outstretched hand. They had addresses and short descriptions of his first post-fireworks assignments—"Injured dog, can't move but won't let anybody near; large dead dog holding up traffic at 3rd and Wall (downtown); injured dog (minor) from two-vehicle accident, pick up at South Precinct." After he left the building, I went to the kennel area and picked out a puppy to keep me company for the rest of my shift—a dose of much-needed dog medicine.

Michael and I never talked about what happened to him that night. We didn't talk much at all after that. I wanted to say something to him, but anything I could think of to say seemed too personal or too dumb. He pointedly avoided talking about it. We steered clear of one another, friends no more. Within a few months he quit working for Animal Control and went back to school. Eventually I learned about post-traumatic stress disorder (PTSD), so-named in 1980 by the American Psychiatric Association. It took some time for the newly named disorder to become commonly known, but as soon as I read about the disorder in some newspaper article, I recognized Michael's behavior for what it must have been, a flashback from his time in the Vietnam war.

Years later, I heard that Michael finished a degree in psychology and became a social worker and counselor. He married and had two children. Every July 4th I think of him and wish him well. Since that holiday night, I've learned more about PTSD. I've seen some more of the damage it's done—to people in general, to friends and relatives—and to some animals. Dogs can suffer behavior changes as a consequence of fireworks or other trauma. Michael recovered enough to go on and make a good life.

Nowadays dogs are commonly recognized as good medicine for veterans suffering from PTSD. Service dogs alleviate anxiety and help people cope with the aftereffects of war and other psychic wounds. I have hated the noise of fireworks, even on television, since that night. When July 4th comes around, I take my dog and head for some quiet place.

CHAPTER II

ROMAR KENNELS

After high school, I moved to the San Francisco Bay Area. My first official self-acknowledged actual lesbian girlfriend, Jan, and I needed to move from our little house in San Rafael because the landlord died unexpectedly. I had the little West Highland White Terrier puppy she had bought for me—saying she thought the beautiful little animal was the perfect match for me. Jan said it all so romantically. We named the little dog Tager, somehow derived from William Blake's poem "Tyger, Tyger, burning bright/In the forests of the night...." We had also taken custody of a cat that the previous tenant of our house had abandoned.

Tager, the cat, Cilla, and I needed new lodgings, because Jan wanted to move back to her parents' house in Pomona and go to the University of California at Irvine. The puppy was to keep me from being lonely. Jan's parents' house was too tiny for all of us and she couldn't afford to live anywhere else. I still had a job in San Francisco as a bank teller. Our separation would be temporary, but "Separate we must, for the time being. It's for the best," she said. It *was* for the best. I had more lessons to learn out in the world.

The house remained ours for another two weeks. I

searched for a place to live that would accept the animals. While looking through want-ads, I also searched for a new job. Working as a bank teller at the Hong Kong and Shanghai Banking Corporation in downtown San Francisco wasn't happy-making. I deeply hated working there.

My high school experience working with English Setters gave me the confidence to apply for a job I saw advertised in the San Rafael Independent Daily Journal: "Live-in kennel attendant. Experience caring for dogs in a kennel setting desired. Excellent work ethic required." Lodgings and employment dilemmas solved all at once if I could land the kennel job. Dogs. Yes! I called the number in the ad and made an appointment to visit Romar Kennels, to interview for the position.

Finding the Kennels wasn't difficult, but making my 1958 two-door Fiat 600 go up the steep driveway was difficult. We barely made it. Margo (the "mar" part of Romar) was on her porch waiting for me, not smiling. She was a tall, athletic looking woman with short gray hair, wearing black jeans and a neat checkered shirt. She didn't bother with pleasantries. "Go ahead and bring the dog in." I had Tager with me. She gestured for me to follow her into the house, where we sat at a small round table in the big, old-fashioned kitchen.

After we sat, she wasted no time beginning the interview questions. She asked one question after another, leaving time for short answers only, no chit-chat. "Have you worked with animals? Are you strong enough to spend the whole day at physical labor? This job is not physically easy. Are you dependable? Do you keep your word? Will you mind being away from friends and family? This is a live-in job, you know...." I inserted short answers and after the last question, Margo said, "When can you move in?" I was slightly stunned. Coming to the interview, I thought I would be checking the place out to see if I wanted to do the job, and I assumed my interview was one of many. Surely more people had answered the ad—but I was the one. The one of one or the one of many, I never knew. She hired me without giving me an opportunity to ask questions of her, and I said yes anyway. I gave my two weeks' notice at the bank.

Neither Robert nor Margo wasted any time with small-talk. They had plenty to keep them busy every minute of every day. Both were people who lived for their animals. They had dogs, cats—a wolf—and three stunning Morgan horses. Besides running the large boarding kennel business, they practiced the art of dressage with the horses every morning and they bred and showed their pack of Norwegian Elkhounds. Later, I learned that they had 80 acres of forest somewhere, a two-hour drive, which they made every other weekend. They were building a retirement home for themselves.

My job was a little daunting at first, but I could wear overalls and work with dogs. Heaven. My employers didn't mind my bringing Tager and the calico cat Cilla. I hoped that I would become accustomed to the physical labor before it killed me. I thought I was in decent shape for a former bank teller. I didn't die. Muscles and stamina happened. The Romar property was beautiful, a perfect getaway from real life, which I found to be prickly and emotionally exhausting.

The experience at Romar still comes back to me occasionally, sometimes with a smile, but often with a pin-prick of regret. Working there nudged me closer to the path that I might not have followed if not for my experiences there. I learned valuable things about animals, people, the value of hard work, the value of solitude. I also learned something about wolves.

Robert and Margo Ransom were the long-time owners of Romar Kennels—Ro for Robert and mar for Margo. The property consisted of eight acres on a grassy hill with a large, white house at the top where Robert and Margo lived. A half-mile long dirt road ran from the front of the house downhill to a paved road. I didn't try driving my Fiat up the hill again. It stayed parked near the bottom of the driveway. A few yards north of the dirt drive, the land sloped into a deep ravine. The other side of the ravine went up to the property of a curmudgeonly dentist, whose modern house of metal and glass perched at the highest point for miles around.

Below and south of Robert and Margo's house, a U-shaped group of partially covered kennel-runs housed some of their pets, and some special-needs animals, including a big gray wolf named Cissy. This group of kennel-runs was referred to as the "house kennels."

Cissy's original owners got her as a pup, thinking that owning a wolf was chic. However, Cissy grew up, and even though she started out as a cute dog-like puppy, she didn't grow into a fabulous exotic pet as planned and she didn't behave like a dog. She became too difficult for her owners to handle. I never knew the details of her back-story, but her owners had been given a deadline to either find her a new home or have her put down. Robert agreed to take her. He was the only person allowed to take her out of her enclosure. That was one of the rules made clear to me with emphasis when I was hired.

Most of the time Robert and Margo took care of the house kennels, but when they were gone, I sometimes fed Cissy and the other animals in her neighborhood. Robert and Margo's house-dogs were kenneled when their owners were away for more than a day, and all the dogs with medical problems or special needs rotated in and out of the house kennels as necessary. A black Lab named Tally with acute anxiety sometimes stayed in the run next to Cissy. He and the wolf got along well. She seemed to have a calming influence on him. He belonged to a friend of the Ransoms who traveled frequently.

Cissy fascinated me. I saw her infrequently, only when the Ransoms were off to horse shows or dog shows. She was a big, rangy gray wolf, not as beautiful as the ones on TV, but an impressive beast. She had beautiful amber eyes. She didn't look at me with the sweet, fawning dopy look, or the questioning, please give-me-a-job look typical of most dogs. She was more alert, more watchful, more quietly curious, and with no apparent desire to do anyone's bidding. If I didn't know she was a wolf, from a distance I might have guessed that she was a mixed breed, maybe a sled dog, but looking closely, her expression was different from that of a domestic pet. She was friendly enough. She was happy to take treats from me, and she seemed docile. When she interacted through the chain link with Tally, the anxious lab, she was gentle and motherly.

My main job was farther down the hill in one of two long kennel buildings that housed around 20 to 25 boarding dogs each. The long-term and permanent boarders were in my building. I was responsible for keeping the kennel runs and the rest of the building clean and the dogs in it fed, groomed, and exercised. The kennel manager, a strange, surly little woman who liked to be called "Snake," was responsible for the other kennel building. Snake had a great work ethic and she knew every inch of the Ransom property, but she lived off-site in her own house, which was about five miles away from Romar. Besides caring for the temporary boarding dogs in the other kennel building, she sometimes helped the stable hand do whatever the stable hand did. I saw him from a distance occasionally but I only saw him and the lovely Morgan horses from afar.

Snake and I never became friends. I think she tried to make a friendly overture by inviting me over for dinner at her house one evening about two weeks after I began working at Romar. Maybe she was just warning me off. She wasn't easy to read. She had a crew cut and some tattoos, and I thought it a good bet that she was a dyke. We ate spaghetti, with few words exchanged. After dinner we went outside to drink coffee and smoke our after-dinner cigarettes on the porch. We went out there because it was a pleasant summer night, not because she habitually smoked outside. Her house probably reeked of smoke. Maybe the windows were stained brown with nicotine. As a smoker, I didn't notice. Now it's hard to believe that smokers were oblivious to the unpleasant evidence that clung to them and their surroundings (including me and mine).

My preferred smoke was always Marlboro Menthols. Snake's preference was Camels, the kind with no filter. That gesture of picking tobacco off the tongue was so familiar in those days. It was no more attractive then than it would be now. Almost everybody smoked then—in movie theaters, airplanes, offices, even hospitals. During the six years that I smoked, I thoroughly enjoyed my cigarettes and half a century later I still miss them sometimes.

Snake told me without preamble that her girlfriend had left her two years before and that she wasn't looking for another one. I told her I had a girlfriend in LA. She didn't need to worry about me. She showed me the tattoos on her arms. One was a snake. Not a surprise. She was way ahead of her time with the tattoos. She told me she liked to play pool—didn't read much or go to movies. We had nothing in common except the habit of smoking, and we had nothing to talk about except the kennels. After that dinner we avoided any appearance of friendship other than as cooperating co-workers. Although her title was "kennel manager," she wasn't my boss. Margo was. Snake had work ethic down. I admired her dedication.

The Ransoms had the three Morgan horses in a stable next to a training ring where they practiced dressage in the early morning. A few times I got up early enough to watch them practice with the horses. Dressage is enchanting to watch. The horse and rider move as one, with no obvious commands given by the rider. According to a definition from The Free Dictionary online, dressage is "the guiding of a horse through a series of complex maneuvers by slight movements of the rider's hands, legs and weight." It's an art. Most of the time I was too exhausted from the days' labors to get up at 5:30 in the morning with the excessively energetic Ransoms. Occasionally I had some regret about missing the graceful morning performances, but after a hard day of cleaning, feeding and exercising the other inhabitants of my kennel building, sleep came down like a feather dropped in a vacuum, and waking up was like trying to subvert gravity. Placing my alarm clock across the room forced me to get out of bed every morning in time to start my work.

My miniscule apartment was built-in at one end of my kennel building. The walls and ceiling of the apartment were knotty pine. I had room for a twin bed, a small chest of drawers and one chair. The tiny bathroom shared a sink with the kitchen, which consisted of a small cupboard above a narrow counter that held a two-burner hotplate and a toaster oven. Under the counter was the miniature refrigerator. The little space had everything Tager and I needed. During my work hours, Tager stayed in one of the kennels or in the exercise yard—or in the apartment if the weather was bad.

The mostly-gray tortoiseshell cat, Cilla, went in and out a flap inserted in one of the high, narrow sliding windows on the wall above the bed. Sometimes she brought me little snakes as gifts. At first I thought they were dead, but Cilla only knocked them out. When I saw one of them wriggle out of my garbage can, I started disposing of them outside, across the road by the ravine.

Two long-term boarders, Basset Hounds named Cynthia and Abigail, lived on the other side of my apartment wall. They frequently sang the Basset blues—ah-oooo, ah-oooo! I didn't mind at all. They had nice singing voices. Their owners had moved to Europe but couldn't bear to give up the dogs. I was told they visited the Bassets once or twice a year, but I never saw them. The other two dogs that stayed at the kennel for the entire time I worked there were Bucky and Casey, an English Springer Spaniel and an Irish Setter.

I loved walking the aisle down the middle of the kennel building, greeting the dogs by name and telling them whatever I felt like telling them, before I got down to the business of cleaning up. After my blisters turned to calluses and my muscles became accustomed to the work, scrubbing and hosing kennel runs and playing with my four-legged neighbors was way more fun than counting out dollars all day, smiling at people, making columns of numbers balance. Wearing jeans, T-shirts and tennis shoes was bliss compared to wearing girdles, dresses, stockings and heels. Ugh.

Bucky and Casey's owner, Mary Jane, visited her dogs three times during my time at Romar. She was a massively obese woman. She brought her obese female Cocker

Spaniel named Dusty with her when she drove over from San Francisco to visit her boys. The Ransoms said she had "plenty of money" and came from a prominent San Francisco family. The front seat of her station wagon had been replaced by custom-made seat that looked like an upholstered board with a slight dent in it to accommodate Mary Jane's girth and inability to bend enough to sit normally. She wore a garment that looked like two colorful bedsheets sewn together with holes for head and arms. I had never met anyone like her. She was soft-spoken, pleasant and well-educated, introduced by Robert and Margo as a long-time friend. I had a hard time coordinating her personality with her shocking appearance. These days she might be on a reality TV show. I, in my youthful ignorance, couldn't fathom how a person could allow herself to become as large as Mary Jane. Later in life I learned how much suffering happens when a body goes out of control—internal suffering, physical suffering, all compounded by external lack of understanding, ridicule and censure.

    Mary Jane brought Bucky and Casey boxes full of whole roast chickens, whole roast beeves, boxes of Hershey bars and packages of sliced cheese. Chocolate is poisonous to dogs, but that wasn't common knowledge in 1968. Still, most people understood that chocolate isn't good for dogs. Robert and Margo tried to explain to Mary Jane that they could not possibly feed candy to her dogs, nor would Bucky and Casey be able to eat more than a little bit of the meat and cheese she brought, but she smiled or nodded and seemed to hear none of it. Every time she returned with the same huge quantities of inappropriate food. She insisted on eliciting promises that Bucky and Casey would be able to feast on her gifts. She didn't mind if they shared some of their food with others.

Robert and Margo told me that Bucky and Casey were each 15-20 pounds overweight when the two dogs came to stay at the kennel. When I met them, they were of normal weight, healthy and fit.

The gates to the exercise yard were opened to allow Mary Jane to drive her station wagon inside. While she was visiting, she leaned against her car with Bucky and Casey dancing around her. Dusty the Cocker leaned from side to side trying to dance with her brothers. Mary Jane fed them all some chicken, a few slices of beef and a couple of slices of cheese for as long as she was able to stand up, which wasn't for more than a few minutes. Robert and Margo kept the chocolate out of the way. Robert assisted Dusty into the back of the station wagon as Mary Jane rolled into her custom-made driver's seat. Robert and Margo gave up trying to reason with her about the food. They always promised that "the boys" would get the very best of care including all the nourishing food and tasty treats they needed, without being specific about the disbursement of Mary Jane's well-intentioned gifts. I sometimes wondered if Mary Jane really intended her food offerings as gifts to us. She had to know that the dogs couldn't eat it all. Maybe she didn't know how to express her appreciation for the care of Bucky and Casey except through food.

When the station wagon was out of sight, the Ransoms let me take what I could use from the huge box of food—a roast chicken, a small package of cheese and a box of Hershey bars fit into my tiny refrigerator. None of the food was wasted. Bucky and Casey and the rest of the long-term boarders received bits of chicken or beef or cheese as treats when they were in the exercise yard for the next few days. Robert and Margo made sure the rest of the food was used or given away.

The dogs in the kennels were fed in the late afternoon. The food consisted of kibble mixed in a cement mixer with bags of chopped beef. The frozen beef came in forty-pound boxes delivered every other week and placed in a walk-in freezer in the shed where we mixed the food. The Ransoms, Snake and I mixed and dished up the meals, which we then delivered to the excited dogs as fast as possible to keep them as quiet as possible.

Besides tending to the kennels, another of my duties had to do with the dentist who lived on the other side of the ravine. He moved into the house he built—over a period of many months—and then decided that the kennels were too noisy. He sued the Ransoms over the noise and he lost. Romar Kennels had been in business for twenty years before the dentist decided to build his house at the top of the hill across the ravine. If he had built his house just 100 feet down the other side of his hill, he would still have had magnificent views and he wouldn't have been in the worst possible place to have the kennel sounds swept uphill toward his house. He built where he wanted, without much forethought.

The dentist's already sour temper wasn't sweetened by losing the court case against Romar. He mounted speakers in his trees to play unpleasant sounds in the direction of the kennels. His loudspeaker noises didn't carry down to the kennels as well as the kennel sounds carried up to his house. The speakers were short-lived. The noises he blasted made the dogs bark more than ever. I couldn't help but enjoy the fact that his revenge backfired so nicely.

Even though the dentist was such a miserable neighbor, we tried to keep the barking at a minimum. The Ransoms wanted to be good neighbors. The best way they found to stop the barking was to pound on the chain link and yell "Quiet!" That action usually distracted the dogs enough to keep them from barking for a while, until something else set them off. When the barking started again, everyone would stop what they were doing to pound chain link and yell "Quiet! Quiet!" I don't know how well the yelling played on the other side of the ravine. At least he could hear that we were trying.

The one unpleasant experience that marks my memories of my time at Romar happened when the Ransoms were away. I was in charge of feeding the animals in the house kennels. I fed Cissy the wolf, as usual. I fed her the same way I fed the other dogs, by opening the kennel door and setting the food down in front of her. She never made an aggressive move. She took her milk bones through the chain link politely, as always. When the animals were through eating, I opened each door and removed the dishes, treating Cissy exactly as I did her neighbors. I felt confident that I could have walked her on a leash with no problem, but I respected the rules.

At some point, the dogs in the house kennels started barking while I was in the process of feeding them. Without thinking, I banged on the nearest chain link gate and yelled "Quiet!" The gate I hit belonged to Tally, the nervous black lab next to Cissy. Poor Tally was startled and ran to the back of his run, whimpering. Cissy suddenly became a real storybook wolf, crouching down, showing her big teeth and growling a wolf growl that is so definitely not the same as a dog growl. I was stricken to be on the bad side of the big gray wolf with yellow eyes and big teeth, especially when I had thought we were friends. Her family of origin was my family fantasy from way back—

raised by wolves.

Tally forgave me immediately, but Cissy and I were never at ease again. When I fed her after that incident, I threw some meat to the back of the kennel, opened the door, and put her dish down before she had time to run back. I wasn't comfortable placing the dish in front of her as I had before. I don't think she would have hurt me, but she would not let me make amends, no matter how many treats I gave or how many apologies I offered. She would no longer take the treats from my hand or eat the ones I dropped on the floor of her kennel until I was out of sight. She never growled at me again, but her changed attitude was evident and made me feel foolish and sad. Romar wasn't as comfortable anymore, because I had underestimated wolf sensibilities and had acted without thinking when I scared poor Tally.

A few weeks later, I took my savings and moved to Southern California where Tager, Cilla and I moved in with my girlfriend, Jan, and her parents. The house was tiny. I slept on a couch. Jan already had a little poodle, so the house was crowded with animals, too. Jan's mother fell in love with Cilla. For a few months the household got along very well, until the inevitable breakup happened. Cilla stayed with Jan's mother. Tager and I moved on to further adventures. My experience at Romar became useful when I went to work at Animal Control, and I'll always remember the place as a happy sanctuary, except for the incident with Cissy. The thought of her makes me wince, but I'm glad we met. She taught me that lesson again, about thinking before acting, that I'm still working on. Mastering it is hard, because sometimes acting without thinking works out. Mostly not, though.

CHAPTER 12

HERE KITTY KITTY

The day finally arrived when my promotion to Animal Control Officer Two came through. After two years and one month as a kennel attendant, I advanced to field work. At last I was doing the job I wanted. For the first few months in the field, I rode with an experienced officer to learn how to handle the multitude of details involved in serving the public as an Animal Control Officer. I was eager to learn everything, having heard so many stories from the other field officers about their daily adventures. Officers encountered all kinds of animals in unimaginable situations—not only dogs and cats, but wild animals, exotic birds, farm animals, and humans, who were always completely unpredictable. Some stories were hilarious. Some were exciting. Some were tragic. Some were frightening. None of the stories was boring.

    Mastering the basics didn't take long. We drove trucks with metal cages attached to the chassis, three large cages and three smaller ones on each side, with a big enclosure at the back that opened on both sides. The enclosure at the back was for dead animals. We picked up those, too. My severe squeamishness gave way quickly. Amazing how fast a person can get used to whatever status is the current quo. Scooping up messy remains was by far better than helping the vet to create rows of empty little bodies, no longer part of my assignments. Writing tickets on police ticket books was a novel experience. We enforced a list of regulations under the city's animal ordinance, primarily the leash law. All dogs were required to be on a leash in public areas. Occasionally we witnessed citizens fail to pick up after their animals. People who don't pick up after their dogs really hate being cited for their inconsiderate, unsanitary habits, but it's empowering to be able to do something about those and other transgressions. We were cautioned not to allow our new policing power to get out of hand. Even the power to enforce animal laws could get in the way of reasonable behavior toward the citizens we served. As police officers, we had periodic classes to remind us to be polite and use good sense, no matter what situation we found ourselves in, no matter what kind of unpleasant behaviors we had to endure from people who didn't appreciate our existence. We were dog-catchers, after all, worse in many minds than the lowest of the low.

For the most part, we answered calls about specific animal problems from individuals who phoned the animal control dispatch desk. We picked up stray animals of all kinds, not only dogs and cats. Sometimes we picked up dogs that had bitten people. By law, biters had to be quarantined for two weeks for rabies (although rabies can have a much longer incubation period). We investigated cruelty reports, dog fighting, cock fighting, puppy mills. We took custody of dogs involved in court cases. We issued citations for leash law violations and other violations of the city codes involving animals. Some calls were totally unique and unexpected.

The dispatcher contacted field officers by radio to give us our assignments. Learning the radio codes was fun. I especially liked to say "10-4."

Dispatcher: Hey, Five (our truck number), What's your 20?

Me: 6th and Lark. We're 10-44 (on a break).

Dispatcher: Got a 10-91 when you're done—422 Main St. (stray to be picked up)

Me: 10-4, give us 30 minutes. Dog or cat?

Dispatcher: Yeah, a black lab. I'll let 'em know. 10-4.

I loved talking on the radio. Radio codes made us sound like official officials of the law. Too cool. I carried a personal radio on my belt, a two-pound walky-talky with a short antenna. The belt also had room for a long, heavy flashlight and a nylon leash. We also had 2-way radios in our trucks.

Near the end of my six-month training period, my trainer for the day, Debbie, and I took a call indicating that some new tenants had found a "10-91" (generic stray animal) occupying their new apartment, likely a pet left by the previous tenant. The dispatcher wasn't specific and we didn't ask what kind of animal. We assumed the animal would be the usual sort of abandoned pet, a dog or a cat. The dispatcher didn't say otherwise.

Debbie was a big, tall red-head who had been a field officer for about five years. She was a great mentor, with a formidable presence and a lot of experience. Among other things, she demonstrated the best professional demeanor to maintain while issuing a leash-law-violation ticket. I don't recall anyone who was happy to receive a ticket. Some people laughed and couldn't believe we were enforcing "such a ridiculous law." Some were angry. A few were contrite and another few were threatening. Suzanne powered through the process without a smile and without responding to any threat, argument or angry question. When she handed over the ticket, she was unfailingly polite, no matter the recipient's attitude. I had to work a bit at emulating her silent aplomb, but I mastered it and after writing a few tickets, I felt like I earned my badge. We had police badges. Under the city's employment structure, we were indeed police officers. Suzanne helped adjust my mindset so that I felt the authority of the badge without forgetting that my job was a service to the public, no matter how the public felt about it. She had a great teacher's talent for passing along her expertise, tips and tricks for handling different kinds of situations. I liked and respected her.

When we arrived at the address where we were to pick up the abandoned pet, three young men, probably students, were standing among stacks of moving boxes near the porch of their new apartment, which was in an upscale neighborhood near the University. None of the three was entirely coherent, but we gathered from their gestures and squeaks that there was a snake in the bathroom of their new apartment. "A snake. Funny. Thanks, Dispatch." Debbie spoke into her portable radio as we walked toward the apartment.

I was excited to see what we would find. I took the lead going into the apartment, as the boys retreated farther from the door yelling cautions. I assumed that Suzanne was behind me and would know what to do. Snake calls were rare. In fact, I had never heard anybody talk about dealing with snakes, but I knew reptiles of all kinds were kept as pets by some reptile aficionados. I had seen all kinds of snakes in terrariums in pet stores, but I didn't know much about them. Snakes are animals; I assumed there was some protocol at Animal Control for dealing with them.

The front door clicked shut, and I heard Debbie's footsteps pass behind me as I cautiously opened the bathroom door. There it was, a big, beautiful constrictor of some kind, coiled beside the vanity. I went in and squatted down to get a better look. The snake was stunning, with dark blue and cream patterns running its length, perfectly coiled in a wide cone shape with its head at the top, raised and looking at me. It showed no sign of aggression. I looked at Debbie, who was standing a few feet back from the bathroom door. "What are we supposed to do with this guy?"

Debbie took another step backward, looking pale and horror-stricken. She said in a small voice, "Here, kitty kitty?"

We didn't laugh about her response until later, when some of her color returned. I was evidently completely on my own this time. Every day we had different experiences. This was a new one for both of us. I had no history at all with handling snakes, but I wasn't afraid of the one in front of me. I knew the difference between constrictors and poisonous snakes. This one had been someone's pet. How dangerous could such a beautiful creature be? I knew constrictors could bite, but they didn't usually bite unless provoked. Provoking wasn't my intention. I reached for the snake, grasping it behind its head as I had seen animal handlers do on television. The poor abandoned creature seemed grateful for a friendly presence. The snake surprised me by quickly coiling all of its four-foot length around my arm. I was charmed. Carrying it outside I tried to look professional rather than triumphant. The boys shouted, "Thank you!" from a distance. The snake, now known as "Kitty," stayed happily where it was, snugly (but not tightly) wrapped around my arm. Debbie drove us back to the shelter without saying much except, "Nice job." From that day on, I was the designated snake officer and no longer a trainee.

No one came to claim the beautiful snake. Three days later, I took it to the Woodland Park Zoo, where one of the keepers identified it as a Ball Python with unusually spectacular markings. The zookeeper assured me that the animal would find a comfortable home, if not with the zoo, then in a place with people who were responsible and knowledgeable about snakes. I was happy to leave Kitty in good hands.

CHAPTER 13

MY MOTHER

I have wondered about how my mother's background affected our relationship. Becoming reacquainted with her after a 30-year hiatus has made me re-open childhood memories. My turning to the dogs for sustenance had something to do with her. I think. Or maybe I was born with the mother-loving screw loose. In second grade I realized that I didn't love my mother. No one else said that. I didn't suppose anyone thought it except me, and I didn't say it. I made the obligatory handprint and macaroni gifts. I made cards for Mother's Days. Maybe I was fitted with some misplaced screws, thus making canines feel more like family than family.

I knew Mom wasn't impressed with the handprints or the macaroni, though she made an effort. She seemed to be tight-lipped and angry or distracted when I was around. Of my gifts she typically said something like, "That's nice, Sweetie. Don't leave it there. Put it in your room." She wasn't a terrible horrible person. We didn't click, we didn't bond in the early years, which didn't bode well for the years that came after.

I suspect my mother's childhood, as well as our English stiff-upper-lippy cultural roots, had a lot to do with why she kept me at a distance. In her own beginnings, she had a damaged connection or two that messed cruelly with her own family ties. She was born tone-deaf and completely without a sense of rhythm to a pair of musical vaudeville entertainers. Her parents didn't understand how such a thing could happen. They didn't believe it for a long time and kept trying to find some music where none existed, making my mother try and inevitably fail over and over.

Nanny, my mother's mother, was a charming, beautiful, sweet, sheltered woman. She was pampered all her life by her six older brothers, by her strong, opinionated mother, and by my Grampy. She first sang onstage when she was four years old. Everybody who knew wonderful, talented, adorable "Little Millie" loved her, for all of her life. She always depended on her charm to move her through the world. As far as I know, it never failed her. She never learned to drive a car, and she didn't care to cook. She baked cakes and pies sometimes, and she cleaned like a demon, but Grampy took care of the shopping and cooking and most everything else. On a limited income, they still managed to get out and mingle frequently, enough to be footnoted in the society pages every once in a while. The only shopping Nanny did was for clothes, for herself and for me.

My mother shared a love of fashion with Nanny. They both loved looking "smart" and "well-put-together," and they loved to dress me. Bargain racks held no treasure they didn't find. None of the rich kids looked better than I did in my school wardrobe shopped for in The City (San Francisco) every summer.

When my mother was born, Nanny was sick with puerperal fever and the after-effects for more than a year. During that time she had a live-in nurse to care for her and the baby. As the baby—my mother—began to grow, and my grandmother got better, the nurse went away. My docile grandparents then took a backseat as parents to Nanny's mother, my great-grandmother, Emily, who lived with them. Great Grandmother Emily was so stern and opinionated that my grandfather called her "The General." She was a staunch Anglican who made it clear that she could not stand Catholics, "those ungodly idol-worshiping papists." The Irish Catholic family next door was apparently an exception. The General lavished baked goods on them and allowed my mother to babysit for their many little ones.

The General almost always wore black. She was a widow, like Queen Victoria. She was small in stature like the Queen, but large in presence. Nothing about her was sweet or warm or amenable to change according to my mother—although my Nanny remembered her mother as strong and caring, if a little over-protective. Grampy got along well with his mother-in-law. He was fine with letting her rule the household. She didn't mind being called The General by her son-in-law. "Yessir, General Ma'am. As you wish." Ken Chapman was as charming as his lovely wife, Milly, and he was handsome, with twinkling blue eyes.

The General believed that girls should be taught womanly arts. Her granddaughter should be able to sing, or at least play the piano, but my mother didn't have any music in her. The General took years of convincing that musicality cannot be forced. After dismally failing at singing lessons, Mom had piano lessons, and then other music lessons, but lessons were only painful for everyone involved. Dancing lessons were even more dismal. At last, the General gave up on music and settled on elocution lessons. My mother learned to recite like a champ. She still says to-mah-to and cahn't. Eventually she found that she had a talent for acting and performed a few times with a local theater group, but she had to give it up when she realized she couldn't do everything she wanted as a divorcee with a child. She had artistic talents, but nothing she produced pleased her and she discarded her brief pursuits one by one—drawing, painting, knitting, sewing, macramé, cross-stitch…. After one or two creations in each medium, she put each away without looking back. I thought her few drawings and paintings were wonderful. The sweater she knitted for me had arms that reached almost to my knees, but I wouldn't let her throw it away. I wore it for years. The flannel nightgown she made me as her one and only sewing project stayed with me for years, too.

The General died when my mother was sixteen years old, after high school graduation and shortly before my mother entered the University of Nevada (She still says Nev-ah-da, which is incorrect as most true Nevadans know). She told me that she felt as if shackles had been removed when she left home to live in her sorority house and she "went a bit wild." She was married and pregnant (or pregnant and married) by the time she was eighteen.

Nanny and Grampy, loved their only child, but I see how they might not have been blue-ribbon parents to my mother. When I was a little girl, they took me on vacations with them, often to San Francisco where we mixed shopping for school-clothes with afternoons of musical theater. We went to the World's Fair in Seattle and to Disneyland and down the California Coast. In San Francisco and Seattle, Nanny and I always went to the theater. Grampy always got us seats down front, close to the stage. When we saw "Hello, Dolly" with Ginger Rogers, I wondered why Ginger's hands were so wrinkled when her face was smooth. We were a little too close to the stage for that play.

Grampy didn't go with us to the theater. He preferred going to the races, but after the show, or after a day of clothes-shopping, we all went to one or another of the finest restaurants in town. We talked about the show, the food, shopping....

My grandparents were good to me. I loved them, but we seldom touched one another, and never hugged. They almost never talked about their own histories or anything personal. We expressed affection through the medium of dogs. During the time we had our first family dog, Boulou, they had a black setter-mix named Tippy. Every day Grampy took Tippy to the Dairy Queen for an ice cream cone. When I was at their house, I went along with Grampy and Tippy to the Dairy Queen. The dog always sat in his usual place in the front seat. I sat in back. My cone was dipped in chocolate. Tippy had to settle for unadorned vanilla.

Mom and I seldom approved of one another. Sometimes we agreed on clothes, but my memory of her younger face never has her smiling. Tight-lipped disapproval is the face that my childhood memories conjure. I don't remember her ever smiling lovingly, or gushing over any of my accomplishments or saying "I love you." She didn't sit with me when I was sick. From what I learned from the elementary school grapevine, mothers always attended lovingly to their sick children. Backs and tummies were rubbed. Vicks VapoRub was applied to congested little chests. Nope. Not in our house. Mostly I rubbed my own Vicks. Mom gave me the blue jar, but she didn't stay for the caretaking rituals.

Once Mom came to sleep with me in my bed when I was hallucinating with a high fever. Dad wasn't home for some reason. He usually did some sort of kind, awkward, patchy job of dealing with my childhood illnesses—

measles, mumps, chicken-pox, flu—if he was around. When Mom reluctantly came to my bed, probably because I wouldn't calm down, she and I didn't cuddle. She didn't say sweet things. She pushed me away because I was "too hot." She was a smoker and she had bad breath. I think we were both relieved when she went back to her own bed. My stuffed animals were more reassuring.

I didn't approve of my mother, any more than she approved of me. None of my knowledge about her upbringing explains why she dyed her hair red when I was seven or eight years old. I was totally mortified when she came home looking like I Love Lucy. Where I learned to think that dyed hair was practically a mortal sin is a mystery. My impression is that I learned to dislike dyed hair, especially red hair, from my mother, but that shouldn't be right. She wore her hair in a "French Roll" sometimes, which was a fashionable, sleek hairdo for a respectable legal secretary, but I hated the color. She should have been embarrassed to be so brazen. (I had an excellent vocabulary for my age and knew what "brazen" meant.) I may even have thought she was acting like a hussy. I can't have learned to be such a prudish little girl from anyone other than my mother.

Thinking back, I know Mom had a deeply puritanical side to her, but she also wanted to be noticed and she wanted to have fun. She wanted to be free from the tightly structured religious beliefs that she grew up with, so much so that she became a dedicated atheist. I think she disapproved of her prudish self, but it came out in her parenting anyway. And it came out in me, like some other recognizable behaviors have turned up in me. I can carry a tune, but I didn't sing out loud in front of anybody until I was in my forties. I danced at some high school dances, copying my peers out of sheer social necessity, but dancing has never been comfortable. I'm not good at it except in my head. I only dance when no one is watching. I have never and will never dye my hair red, though.

Much later in life I discovered that I do love my mother, more and more as I have gotten to know her. She was 85 years old when she and I became acquainted with one another after a long hiatus. I've recently wondered more than ever about what went so wrong with our mother-daughter bondless relationship. We were completely estranged for close to 30 years before I sent her flowers on her 85th birthday.

Mom never gave me any grief over my being gay. She says she knew before I did. All she said on the subject was that she was sorry that I would probably have a harder time getting along in the world than I would if I were heterosexual. She agrees that she was not a perfect mother to me, but she had a some fine moments. I have to admit that I was not always the easiest daughter either. Now we are the best of friends, and we talk about our pasts as if we never lived in the same universe. She doesn't remember many of the major events of my childhood that I recall, but she remembers events involving me that I don't remember at all. One thing she remembers that may or may not be significant is that when I was a baby, I looked so much like my philandering biological father that they called me "Little Jimmy."

Mom and I have considered that maybe the dog-loving gene was somehow connected to the music gene, and she was born without either. She admits to thinking some dogs are cute. She likes to have music playing in her car. Her car radio is often tuned to a heavy-metal oldies station. Her experience of dogs and music lacks color, or joy or something indescribable. The heavy-metal oldies would be a funny choice for an octogenarian if it weren't sad. I feel bad for the things she's missed and for the things she and I missed together. Now I have more context for her less-than-joyful parenting style. She gets credit for being a sheltered only child who gave birth to me while she was still a teenager. I didn't emerge from the womb with instructions and she was short on experience—a common enough phenomenon, but we must have been allergic to the circumstances. They swelled to uncommon proportions.

The thirty-year estrangement from Mom allowed me to see her as a person instead of as the mother I remembered. She had changed and she was the same. I had a lot of therapy (and exposure to a lot of dogs) and I was the same. We are both senior citizens now. I thank the gods for the canines that helped me navigate my life and ultimately helped make it possible for me to see my mother in a new light. She is smart, funny and says all the right things about politics. Now we can laugh together, groan together over CNN, and laugh some more. I'm still pretty sure we won't cry together. We've had the opportunity, talking about my father for instance. He died of cancer on Christmas Day in 2006. I didn't know he had died until 2014. Both Mom and I still swallow the opportunity for a good cry until we're alone. We carefully pick what we say about Dad, making it matter-of-fact, even though the fact that I missed his long illness and death was a big deal. It is for me a massive regret. I'm sure that my absence at that time confirmed for everybody that I no longer existed as part of the family. Nobody tried to get in touch with me after the last phone call in which I suggested we should stop trying to have a relationship and my mother heartily agreed. Boom. Thirty years of silence.

My brother Keith was angry with me when I first came back, because he "could have used a sister" during my father's illness and death. I think he has gradually gotten over his anger. We're still getting to know each other. I watch "The Walking Dead" on television so that we'll have something to talk about. He's not much of a conversationalist, but he loves to watch that show and I find to my surprise that I've come to like it, too. Nothing like an apocalypse to keep a conversation fresh. He's still my baby brother—stoic, accepting, easy-going.

CHAPTER 14

BUSTER BEAN AND MIDGE, ET AL.

After Boulou died, I still had the support of a dog, although he belonged to someone else. Buster Bean introduced himself. He was a big, furry, gray and white husky-sheepdog mix who appeared one day in the unfenced yard of a house that my friends and I passed on the way home from Peavine Elementary School. As third-graders, we had moved to the newly built Peavine Elementary school half-way through the school year. We were no longer taking a bus to and from the opposite end of town. Peavine School was about a mile downhill from where we lived. My neighborhood friends and I walked home past Buster Bean's house every school day.

Buster B's house was half-way up the hill toward home. We learned his name from the tag on his collar. He never followed us up the hill, but he was beside himself with joy when we paid attention to him. We felt like we were the most important people in his day. We were amazed that he never set foot beyond his front yard, even though he was free. Naturally, we tried to get him to come with us. "Here, Buster. Come on, Boy. Come on. You can do it." We tried tempting him with treats, but he stayed at the edge of the sidewalk stepping up and down with his front feet and making noises that sounded like pleas for us to be reasonable. "Yow wow ooo row you!"

I would have liked to ask Buster's people how they convinced him to stay in his yard, but we never saw anyone come or go from his house. Nobody discouraged us from going onto the lawn to hug and play with their happy huggable dog. We stopped to absorb some of his pure joy almost every day after school.

Sometime during the summer after school ended, Buster suddenly disappeared, taking his joyful elixir with him. Someone said his people moved away. No one seemed to know them.

During the summer I had seen him only when I passed his house in a car. Sometimes I was too preoccupied to look for him, but when I noticed he was gone, my friends and I went to look for him, all of us feeling guilty that we had neglected him all summer. We knocked on the door of the house where he lived, but no one answered. A sign in the window said, "For Rent." I felt his loss as a physical ache and noticed the ache every time we passed his house for a long time, even after another dog came to live with my family.

Shortly after the next school year began, my father convinced my mother to allow me to keep a miniature dachshund puppy offered by a friend, for free. Mom wasn't too happy about it, but she let me keep the puppy. I swore I would feed and water and clean up after her. "I will. I promise. She won't be any trouble. Really. And I'll train her and besides, she's so little you won't even notice her...." Mom ignored me with a sniff, as if to dismiss my claim and at the same time make it clear how magnanimous she was to allow us to take the little dog.

Midget, called Midge, lived mostly in our fenced back yard. She also spent time running around the neighborhood when the weather was reasonably good. She spent as much time in the house as I could manage without being caught. A doghouse for a bigger dog stood in our back yard. She never went near it, as far as I could tell. The warm cement of the patio served as her favorite place in good weather. In bad weather, if I couldn't sneak her indoors, she stayed on the porch in her padded basket. Sometimes we played with her in the yard, marveling at her long silky ears and her comical sausage-shape in motion. We tried to get her to fetch, but she didn't want to go away from us and we usually ended up fetching the toy we had thrown across the yard with her running at our heels. My father laughed, "She's got you kids trained up pretty well."

Sometimes I put Midge in the back of my little brother Ken's stroller when we went for walks. She was cuter than any other puppy could possibly be. My brother was adorable, too, in his striped shirt and red vest. Back then we weren't so fearful of strangers, partly because all the strangers we met in our new subdivision at the edge of town were people just like us—white middle and working-class families. We talked to everybody. I loved the attention, buffered by my adorable companions. Normally people I didn't already know made me nervous. Meeting new people was a chore except when I walked with Ken and Midge. Practically everyone we passed as we walked through the neighborhood stopped to exclaim over the puppy or my brother or both. Meeting strangers that way was almost pleasant.

We didn't "coddle" dogs 60 years ago. Spaying and neutering dogs wasn't common. I wanted Midge to have puppies. My parents seemed to think it was inevitable that she would have puppies. Having her spayed was too expensive. They grumbled about the prospect of puppies, but nobody doesn't like puppies and nothing was done to prevent nature from having its way.

The dachshund down the street was my choice for a sire, but Midge must have had other ideas—at least I wanted to think she had some choice in the matter. My next-door neighbor, Julie, and I put the boy dachshund, Fritz, in our back yard while Midge was in heat, but a yellow lab from parts unknown followed her scent, jumped our fence and impregnated my tiny dog. Julie and my other neighborhood friends and I chased the lab away whenever we saw him. We didn't think he would actually be able to mate with Midge. He was so big, and she was so little. We figured Fritz's seeming lack of interest was modesty. He probably wanted a little privacy. We left them alone in the yard as much as possible. Fritz went back to his own home every afternoon. We had no idea that the lab had succeeded where Fritz failed until Midge's pups were born.

I noticed that Midge's belly became extraordinarily big, but she was a very small dog. I thought she probably had a whole bunch of puppies in there. Nobody else seemed to be overly worried, so I didn't worry either.

After about two months, Midge gave birth alone at night in the dog-house. The morning after the birth, I looked for her everywhere when she failed to come running at my call. Finally, I thought to look inside the doghouse she had always ignored. She had chosen the doghouse as her birthing place. Two of her three extra-large puppies were dead, still covered in the membranes in which they had been born. Little Midge, looking worn out, was licking a third pup that was almost a quarter of her size. That one was alive. My heart cracked but didn't have time to break. The puppy that lived was kicking its little yellow legs as its mother washed every inch of its little yellow body.

The dead puppies were a horrible kind of grim tragedy I had never experienced before. This was death—up close. My Dad helped me bury the cold, stiff little bodies wrapped in a white dish-towel. He dug a hole under the forsythia bush in the back yard. Dad acted as if this kind of thing wasn't as horrible as I thought it was, and he said Midge had no time to be sad over her lost babies. "Dogs almost always live their lives paying attention to what comes next. People spend time worrying about the past, but Midge won't. She's taking good care of her one puppy and she's a happy mama. We'll be sad for a little while, though. People can't help it. The puppies are going back to the earth, and next spring they'll be part of the forsythia bush. You'll see. It'll bloom bigger and better than ever."

I believed my Dad. He didn't spend a lot of time talking with me, but when he did, he said things that usually made sense and made me feel better. After the burial, Mom and Dad had some kind of disagreement about burying the pups in the yard. I think it had to do at least partially with his allowing me to participate in the burial. Mom thought I was too young and the whole thing was too horrifying for me to deal with at such a tender age. I didn't find it horrifying, just sad, and the forsythia bush was spectacular the next spring.

Midge taught me things in her short life. All of my animal friends gave lessons of one sort or another. Hers included things about death, tragedy and heartbreak. She was an exuberant and loving little dog, as most dogs are.

Her oversized puppy, named Mike, received the best possible mothering, worthy of her canid ancestors.

Mike was almost the same size as his mom by the time he was eight weeks old. I learned that we were lucky Midge lived through the birth of her giant pups. Julie's mother said that the little dog shouldn't have been left alone to give birth and hinted that the dead pups might have been saved if the inexperienced mother dog had received some assistance. I think now she was referring to the adults who should have known. At the time, I was devastated to think I might have saved the other puppies. Some of the more complex feelings that life offers were introduced to me through that experience, but I didn't share them with anybody, not even with Midge. I think Julie's mother's words made me extra vigilant around animals and humans, because mistakes are easily made. Julie's mother's few memorable words had a long-term effect. I suspect that a bit of the rest of my life has been spent attempting to make up for the childish ignorance that I once believed was responsible for the deaths of those puppies.

Midge was less than two years old when she left us. We had recently moved to a larger house in another new subdivision because another little brother came along, Keith. We needed more room. The new house didn't have a fenced yard, not that Midge had always been confined in the back yard at our other house. Most dogs roamed freely around the neighborhoods, but they were always home for dinner. We moved to the new house before the neighborhood had completed landscaping. Midge rambled outside every day. No one considered there might be risks. Our back yard was cleared desert scrub that backed up to uncleared desert scrub that continued up into the foothills below Peavine Mountain. Mountain lions and coyotes were seen beyond the edge of the subdivision. We were encroaching on their territories.

In the end neither the mountain lions nor the coyotes took her. Dad said Midge was hit by a car. I think she might have been hit by his car as he was pulling into the garage, but I didn't consider that possibility until later. That day Dad came inside through the door to the garage, and I knew immediately that something horrible had happened. He was crying. I went to the door and saw Midge's body lying near the washing machine. She looked like she was asleep, except for the dark stain under her head. I had never seen my dad cry before. He pulled me away from the door, closing it hard. "Midge has been hit by a car. I'm sorry, Sweetie, she's dead." I ran to my room. That's how it was done. Get the big messy feelings away to solitary confinement.

When a dog dies, people often grieve louder and harder than they do for dead people. In my family we always went to be alone with big feelings. Big feelings were embarrassing and not to be shared. Sharing bad feelings just made everybody feel worse (was the prevailing idea). Sharing good feelings or happy incidents with too much fervor could be seen as boasting. We wouldn't want to do that, either.

Dad took Midge out to the desert to bury her. I saw him from my bedroom window carrying her away toward the foothills, and ran out to go with him, but he was adamant that I stay home. I hated him for not letting me help bury my dog. I'm sure he was doing his best to follow Mom's rules, but at the time I thought he was being a hypocritical monster. I cried in my room and stayed there for most of two days. Mom brought me food. She almost seemed as if she wanted to say something but nothing came out. She was at the end of her maternity leave, hating being cooped up at home with me and my little brothers, and she had no idea how to cope with her feelings about that, let alone about the dog dying. Midge was just gone—no forsythia to memorialize her, which made her loss harder to endure.

Mom totally fell for the notion that females are the weaker of our species and need protecting from the ickier things in life. She believed she was protecting me. She was fearful of melodrama, death, blood, medical procedures, eye drops, bugs, other peoples' opinions.... She never wanted to be a stay-at-home mother, no matter that stay-at-home moms were the ideal. She could have been a little afraid of her children, too.

In the motherhood department, mine was willing to break with convention. She loved her job as a legal secretary. She worked for a federal court judge by the time Keith was born. As soon as she could get back to work, she hired another babysitter for us and set out for the courthouse every morning. Dad worked from dawn until after dusk selling cars. I played with my friends, talked to the babysitter du jour, read books. I stayed angry with Dad for a long time. Not being able to bury Midge did not ruin my childhood, but letting me see her final resting place would have been the right thing to do. (I'm a little angry even now as I write this. He shouldn't have followed ALL of Mom's stupid rules, says the prepubescent voice in my head.)

CHAPTER 15

JUST DOG

After Midge died and after another summer ended, I went back to school, where life was always more interesting and distracting than it was at home. School was always a salvation. Friends, schoolwork and activities pushed grief to the side, but I was continually aware of the absence of canine in the house. We had a series of interesting babysitters though.

A babysitter came in the morning to stay with the boys and was there when I came home from school. She left when Mom came home from work. The first babysitter, LaVerne, loved Elvis Presley. I thought he was awful and had never met anyone who expressed a serious appreciation for him. My mother thought he was terrible, a bad influence, silly, and obscene. I liked talking about Elvis with LaVerne. She was nice. She said Elvis had a beautiful voice. He moved to the music, but he most certainly was not obscene—just very sexy. LaVerne was fired when Mom found out she had been in prison before she became our babysitter, but not before I had already acquired an illicit fondness for Elvis.

The next hire was Marlene, a teenager from Texas. She had a friend, an older woman named Gerry, who came to our house to visit Marlene sometimes and brought beer. I let it slip one day about Gerry and the beer. At about the same time Mom found out that Marlene was an under-age runaway. She said she was eighteen, but she was really only sixteen. She stopped being our babysitter. I liked both Gerry and Marlene. They were nice enough. They gave me my first sip of beer.

After that we had Essie, an older lady who was blind in one eye. She could be impatient and growly with us, but she made lemon pies and home-made noodles and other goodies that almost made up for her prickly attitude. She did not like Elvis, had not been in prison and she wasn't on the run. She stayed for a bit longer than her predecessors.

I found a stray dog. He was a long-haired, black and brown very mixed breed who was scared of many things. We named him Flap. We were going to find him a good home. Essie didn't like him much, but we knew to keep him away from her and he was compliant. He didn't stay with us for long. He was so afraid of being brushed that he screamed if anyone came near him with any implement that looked anything like a brush. Other than his phobic fear of brushes and some other unfamiliar things, he was the quintessential loving family dog.

Flap allowed my brothers to grab and pat and push and roll on him without so much as a hint of irritation. We were not planning on keeping him, according to my mother, although she was softening toward him because of his sweet nature. We couldn't brush him or clean him up to make him more appealing, so Mom decided to take him to the vet to be groomed. He never came back. The vet said he probably had a heart attack. He may have died of fright. At first, Mom seemed almost as broken-hearted as the rest of us when Flap didn't come home, but she bounced back quickly. "I don't want to hear any more about it. He's gone. We can't get him back and that's that."

Nothing was really right without a dog. Losing an animal is excruciating, but I always knew that having a dog was worth the inevitable heartache. I was a bit of a nutcase without the steadying influence of a canine. I was okay at school, but out of school I spent an inordinate amount of time being afraid of things myself—afraid of being alone, afraid of illness, afraid of my own feelings—sometimes heart-pounding fear of nothing nameable—and sometimes afraid of people who required kisses and/or hugs. We didn't practice hugging at home but there was a nightly ritual of kissing on the lips before I went to bed. I didn't do it right. I didn't like it and I never got the hang of the right pressure, or the right pucker. It didn't seem like an expression of affection. It was weird. (Some time after I left home—with instruction and practice—I learned the art of kissing and stopped thinking of it as weird.)

On a chilly day in late autumn or early winter of the year of fourth grade, some months after Flap left us, I went to the supermarket with my mother. She didn't take me grocery shopping often. Maybe she had picked me up from a friend's house or from roller-skating or swimming or visiting with a friend. Anyway, on this day, a boy was standing outside the grocery store with a box of puppies balanced on his bicycle seat. He had a sign that said, "Free puppies, part Cocker Spaniel." They were black, floppy-eared, curly and about as big as a pound of butter.

Mom was barely out of the car while I was running as fast as I could, through the remnants of the last snowfall, to see the puppies. By the time she caught up with me I was holding the one I wanted, ready to beg, ready to plead. "I'll take care of him. Pleeeeeese!! I'll feed him. I'll do everything. I'll make money to pay for his food..."

Begging and pleading worked without much fuss (it didn't usually). "Mustn't make a scene in front of the store." She didn't say it, but I could hear it anyway, an unspoken rule that worked in my favor. Mom was probably also feeling sorry for me because of Midge and then Flap, although I'm guessing about that. She was too stiff-upper-lippy to let me know if she felt sorry, and I think she would have denied it if anyone asked. It never occurred to me to ask a personal question about something like that.

We brought home the new puppy with the groceries. Everybody except Mom was excited, especially my grandmother and me and my older younger brother, who was three. He was too young to care about dog names, but my parents and I haggled over names for the new puppy until we finally gave up and called him J.D. for Just Dog. He stayed with my family until he was eighteen years old, more than ten years after I moved away. While I was still living at home, he often listened patiently to frustrated rantings or provided a needed cuddle. Mom took care of him from the beginning, but he didn't change her into a dog-person. She kind of liked him, though. My brothers grew to young adulthood with J.D. always on call.

CHAPTER 16

LITTLE BROTHERS

I can't say that my brothers were more than a little like pets. For some reason I'm tempted to say that they were like pets, but they weren't. They were more like appealing little humans—like little brothers. My place as only child may have been usurped by them, but I was happy to have siblings. I was eight years old when Ken came along, old enough to practice a little mothering myself. If I wasn't very good at it—well—I was eight.

Mom still spent every night putting my hair in pin curls, even with the new baby in the house. Every night I went to bed with criss-crossed bobby pins all over my head. I had been pin-curled since my braids were cut off just before kindergarten. The height of fashion from my point of view has always been weird and uncomfortable. Mom was overly concerned that I be fashionably dressed and coifed. The pin-curl process was miserable. I hated it. Mom was certain that it was absolutely necessary. She appeared to hate the process as much as I did. I complained; she was angry. The evening ritual did nothing to enhance our relationship. I envied my brothers, knowing they would never have to put up with the same tortures girls endured to keep up with fashion. (Dogs never wavered in their devotion and admiration, no matter what I looked like. Another plus for them.)

Eventually I learned to do my own pin curls and never left home with my brown hair in its absolutely straight natural state. Sometime after elementary school, giant curlers became the torture of the day, and I followed right along, trying to sleep on bristled curlers or on hard plastic curlers the size of juice cans. I doubt that I ever went to school after having a good night's sleep; neither did any of my girlfriends. The habit of following the latest trend was ingrained, encouraged and supported by peer pressure, to which I succumbed without too much thought.

When little brother Ken came home, I thought he was the best thing ever. I often fed him his bottle. Later he and I struggled with spoonsful of strained beets and peas and other smashed foods in little glass jars. He was more trouble than a puppy, but I enjoyed him most of the time. Ken took up a lot of my spare time. He was an adorable, happy little guy. Then my brother Keith came along. Keith took up everyone's time. He had some challenges. Diagnosing his difficulties involved a long and arduous trek to specialist after specialist.

Mom had the measles during the first trimester of her unplanned pregnancy with Keith. She was terrified of having a damaged child. I was unaware of how terrified she was through her entire pregnancy. I knew about the measles and about the possibility of the baby having some problem because of the measles (which I, or one of my friends, had probably passed on to my mother). Whisperings about problems with the baby came to my ears occasionally, but I didn't understand the gravity of it all, and I thought having another baby brother would be fun, even if he wasn't perfect—funny looking, buck-toothed, or flat-footed. All okay with me. Keith was supposed to be born around Christmas, near Ken's birthday, which was December 23. He came later than expected. The month of January was hell for both my parents as I remained more or less oblivious to their anxiety, except for sharing their impatience. Keith made his entrance on Groundhog Day, February 2, 1959.

Other than having a rash all over his body, Keith seemed okay. He was allergic to milk. He drank his sustenance from a bottle, like Ken and me, but his body rejected formulas made of cow's milk and goat's milk. After many experimental formulas, he at last was able to digest soy milk. His physical development seemed to be normal, but he didn't talk when he was supposed to. He made noises but his first discernable word, when he was about 20 months old was "Go'dimmit!" After that, my parents realized he had been talking for a while. He only heard the loudest words, so he learned swear words and "No!" which came out as "Oh!" and "Stop it!" which sounded like "top eh." When he moved on to ma-ma and da-da, his communications began to be translatable. His dialect wasn't easy to understand, but I mastered it before my parents did. He called me "Yinna." My parents learned the basics of his early language, but neither was fluent. Doctors thought he was probably a little deaf, but he could hear some things. Testing a toddler for a hearing deficit posed some problems in 1959, especially when the doctors were unable to understand what the patient was saying. Specialists weren't able to define his difficulties with speech and hearing until a Stanford doctor evaluated him and cracked his code.

Keith was totally deaf in one ear and partially deaf in the other. He also had some type of aphasia—a glitch in the way his brain processed information causing problems with communication. The Stanford specialist said he wasn't "retarded," as most other doctors had labelled him.

Every male doctor/specialist who examined him had a different take on Keith's difficulties and none of their findings matched those of the doctor at Stanford who was a woman. She was a rarity among doctors then. Only a small percentage were women. She had to be better than good. Her examination of Keith yielded a description that made sense, and she said his intelligence tested as normal. Finally, my littlest brother received the hearing aid he needed when he was four. He hated it and buried it somewhere in the back yard.

Keith was the center of the universe during his early childhood. Our dog, J.D., was on standby, but he didn't have much of a job while the boys were little—too many people in the way most of the time. Keith wasn't through with testing. He separated blocks of different colors and stacked them in different configurations as requested. He put shaped objects in the correct holes. Tests of his memory indicated he was on schedule or better at recall, although he couldn't look at a picture—of a falling cup or of a car about to hit something—and be able to say what would happen next. The object would break, the car would crash. He couldn't make the connection. He mostly understood what he was told, although he understood better if he was told clearly while he was watching the speaker, but something in his understanding of the world was slightly different from the mainstream.

Ken remained on the periphery, behaving badly at school, getting in trouble at home. He had no interest in Keith's latest diagnostic test, as would be expected at his age. I, on the other hand, was old enough to be fascinated by the whole process of sorting out my littlest brother. I wasn't any help to Ken.

Keith was a patient little guy. He was well-behaved. He went to preschool with deaf children, and he made friends there, using sign language to communicate. He particularly liked one little girl who had big brown eyes. Once when I was with my mother to drop him off at his school, I asked him what he was going to do that day. He said in his strange dialect, "I wan' ga hwin' wi' da gir' wi' op'n ise." (*I want to go swing with the girl with the open eyes.*) I was enchanted by his pronouncements, that one especially. Ken, on the other hand, began acting out in elementary school. He was stubborn, angry, and not as fun as he had been. When I babysat, which I did frequently for both boys, Ken needed to be in sight at all times. Along with everyone else, I spent too much time losing patience with him. Unfortunately, he wasn't one to gravitate to the dog for comfort.

One Saturday when Ken was about seven years old and Keith was four, Ken went to the movies with two or three friends and Mom made him take Keith along. All of the boys joined the long line of movie-goers waiting to get into the Majestic Theater in downtown Reno. Few adults went to the children's dime matinees. Dropping children off and picking them up after the show was a normal routine. Once they were out of the car and headed for the line, the parent-chauffeur of the day felt free to pull away from the curb and head home. The boys moved slowly forward in the long line. When the theater was filled to capacity, the line cut off right before Keith made it inside. Ken had already gone inside with his friends. He didn't notice—or didn't want to notice—that Keith wasn't with them. When Mom went to pick up the kids at the end of the movie, Keith was missing.

My father called the police. My parents called everywhere to try and find him. They scoured all of downtown in the vicinity of the theater. After Keith had been missing for a couple of hours, I decided I needed to do something and began walking the neighborhood looking for him.

When I reached the corner, I saw Keith trudging uphill toward me. He was a little more than a block away. I ran toward him, partly to save him from J.D.'s extreme welcome, mostly because I was so glad to see him. He was batting at the dog, saying "No! No! No!" when I swept him up to safety. He was more of a "dogs-should-be-seen-at-a-distance-and-never-heard" kind of guy. I knew how the dog felt. Friends, neighbors and my parents had all been thinking dark thoughts while they worried and cried and told each other that Keith would be home soon. I ran carrying him home. He was heavy, but he was my brother.

Keith wasn't angry with Ken. He said that when he didn't get into the show, he walked home. That was the only choice he had. He didn't understand what the big fuss was about. He knew his address, but if anyone had asked him, most likely they wouldn't have understood him. Apparently, no one asked. A four-year-old walking alone on the streets of Reno wasn't that noteworthy in the early 1960s. I don't know how Ken was punished for his role in the drama. I'm sure he received some kind of penalty. His side of the story faded from memory. Poor Ken, the unwitting villain.

When I left home at the age of 18, my brothers were eight and eleven. After that, I spent some holidays at home in Reno, but I never got to know them as teen-agers or as adults. My last clear memory of Ken as a child was on a day when I had come home for Thanksgiving. The holiday was over. I was about to leave again, and was busy with friends rather than family. Ken was twelve years old. The police brought him home after he had been picked up with an older boy in an empty apartment in a building under construction. The boys were smoking and playing cards. Our parents sent Ken to bed without dinner, not a common punishment in our house. Our parents didn't know what to do with him. They were mortified, horrified, stunned that their son could do such a scandalous thing. Brought home by the police! Horror of horrors! I felt sorry for him. By that time, I had some realization that Ken hadn't had much time in the spotlight when Keith came along. No wonder Ken did things to get some attention.

I took Ken a piece of pie and sat on the edge of his bed. His eyes were still red from crying. He said, "I want to be Catholic like Joey so I can be good." I made a gesture uncharacteristic of our family—uncharacteristic of me—smoothing his hair from his forehead and touching his cheek. I told him he was already good. My words were probably too brief and inadequate, but he may remember. These days I don't know him well enough to ask. He really was a good-hearted boy.

Ken is a good man, very much like his father, our father, but with a need for perfection and cleanliness that almost borders on obsessive-compulsive. He converted to the Mormon church when he married Cheryl, a Mormon divorcee with two kids (a boy and a girl). Ken and Cheryl had another child—a girl—together. The family eventually gave up the Mormon church, but both daughters married Catholics and converted to Catholicism. How ironic is that?

Keith lives with our 90-year-old mother. He's socially awkward, very literal—gentle, generous and solicitous toward Mom. He has worked in a warehouse for the last 30 years. He has a best friend of more than 30 years, Mark, who lives nearly 200 miles away. Mark is married with an adult son who calls my brother "Uncle Keith." When Keith has time off from work he goes with Mark and

Mark's extended family on trailer vacations. They all have small trailers and they love recreational vehicles of all sorts.

I have only reconnected with my little family of origin in the last few years, because when I gave up trying to communicate with my mother so many years ago, I cut ties with the whole family—and they cut ties with me. I'm just beginning to get to see how my brothers evolved and I'm gingerly making efforts to know them better. They know very little about me, except that I'm the estranged lesbian daughter, technically their half-sister, who has been gone much longer than she was in their lives.

Ken is a grandfather six times over, called "Bumpy" by his grandchildren. Lots of dogs in his tightly knit extended family, which seems to be a closed group. My mother isn't inside the enclosure. She sees her granddaughter and great-granddaughters at some holiday gatherings. Ken shares pictures and brings Mom donuts and they meet for breakfast now and then.

Both my little brothers are senior citizens now. They're solidly themselves. When I last really knew them, they had barely begun becoming who they are. Getting to know them is a slow process. Neither of them knows me, and who knows what they've been told about me through the years. Ken shows me pictures of his children and grandchildren, dogs and grand-dogs, but I don't know if I'll ever meet them. I imagine his wife and children are suspicious and/or disapproving of me. Catholicism disapproves of my kind. They are all "Mary and Joseph" to the total exclusion of "David and Johnathan." We'll see how it goes.

CHAPTER 17

ON BEING A HERO

I loved my job as a field officer for Animal Control in spite of the parts of the job that were heartbreaking and other parts that were unpleasant to differing degrees. Most of my days were exciting, rewarding, entertaining and fun.

As an officer of the law, I wore a badge and carried a ticket book to enforce the law as it pertained to animals. My ticket book, besides being a tool of law enforcement, magnified my persona as the evil dog-catcher in the eyes of certain members of the public, but my fellow officers and I also got to be heroes on occasion.

Every day I woke up wondering what new adventures might happen during the workday. Every day I learned something new, which to my mind is what life's about—learning new things. I found out about animals and animal behavior, and more than I wanted to know about human behavior. Being able to read animal expressions and intentions became a useful skill in many situations. I enjoyed absorbing information about all kinds of different animals, especially how they communicate. Dogs don't hide their feelings or intentions. If you know what to look for, perceiving the difference between a dog that sincerely wants to bite you and one that only wants to look like he wants to bite you can make the difference between a good day and a bad one.

Animal Control maintained a close association with veterinarians all over the city. When I worked the evening or night shift, I often spent time at the emergency vet because most night emergency calls involved injured animals. Sometimes I assisted in treatment of minor injuries if the clinic was busy. Since only one vet clinic was available for 24-hour emergencies in the 1980s, the single veterinarian on duty was usually swamped. Removing porcupine quills, assisting in the splinting of simple fractures, cutting painful mats from the coats of severely neglected animals, and taking care of other relatively minor conditions were common activities for me in the late night and early morning hours while the vet and his technician were busy saving lives. The emergency veterinarian, Dr. Ted, was a hero to animals and to animal owners nearly every night.

Being a hero is gratifying, even on the smallest scale. One of the early times I was lucky enough to save the day was the day I was called to "do something" about a squirrel in someone's house. When I got there, the entire family—mother, father and two young children—was on edge, everybody clucking and pointing at a barricade of furniture and boxes at the entrance to the kitchen. A squirrel had come in through a kitchen window and had been terrorizing the family for hours before they thought to call Animal Control. I went around the outside of the house to a back door in order to enter the kitchen, taking my heavy leather gloves with me. A kitchen window was open about 6 inches. It opened onto the corner of an L-shaped kitchen counter.

The terrified squirrel was on an open top shelf at the far end of one leg of the counter, behind some decorative tableware. Nothing appeared to be broken, but the ceramics were endangered. I opened the kitchen window as far as it would go. The squirrel made little chirps when I moved toward it. As I reached up to move some cups, the squirrel did an end run around a cream pitcher, flung itself onto the counter and ran out the window. Nothing broke. That was it. Instant hero. The mother shed tears of gratitude, and the rest of the family thanked me over and over. Later they sent a thank you card to the shelter saying how wonderful and professional I was and how much they appreciated our services. Members of the public who didn't hate us were generous with their thanks when we helped them out.

Another time I went to a house near a creek near the city limits to capture a rat that had come up through the toilet into the bathroom (yes, that happens). The woman who lived in the house had recently had back surgery. She was unable to bend over or turn her head. She apologized for having to call Animal Control over "something so trivial," but she was physically unable to take care of the problem herself. Not everyone in her situation felt that a rat problem was trivial.

I closed myself in the bathroom intent on capturing the rodent under a three-gallon plastic bucket. My habit was to call all animals "Punkin" as I was working with them. "Come on, Punkin, get out of there. That's it, get in the tub. Hold it! Punkin, hold still! Get back in there!"

Outside the bathroom door I heard the homeowner laughing and saying, "Stop it, stop it! Please! I can't laugh. It hurts!" Luckily, the rat cooperated within a few minutes and I was able to take it away. The woman said, "You're my hero, and you made my day. I was feeling so sorry for myself, but I'm feeling a whole lot better now. Thank you." She brought a card to the shelter, along with a box of cookies, for all of us to share. More than once grateful citizens brought treats to the shelter to thank us for assistance.

Another episode, which could have ended tragically, resolved peacefully because of my experience with and affinity for dogs—and because of a certain amount of grace and more than a little good luck. I was assigned an emergency call: Two large dogs were fighting and no one could get them to stop. Both owners were at the scene. The two dogs had previously been friendly with one another and the owners were afraid that one of them had "gone crazy or had rabies or something."

When I arrived at the complainant's address, I could hear the ruckus coming from the back yard. A neighbor had been sent to wait for me in the front yard. "They're trying to kill each other. I don't think you can do anything. I think they should have called the police, but the police would probably shoot 'em." We went around the house to the enclosed back yard.

Several people were watching the dogs from a distance. At first the dogs looked like they were fighting, but they weren't doing it in the usual way. Both were standing on their hind legs. Their heads were close together whipping back and forth as if they were trying to bite one another but not succeeding. They were making a lot of noise—snarling, shrieking, growling—but neither dog was winning, for sure. The situation looked less and less like a fight as I approached them. Up closer, I could see that the chain collar of one of the dogs was twisted around the lower jaw of the other. They weren't fighting but they were desperate and potentially dangerous.

People behind me were talking over one another, saying how the dogs had always been so nice and friendly. They had lived next door to one another for a long time. I took hold of the collar of the dog who had the chain wrapped tight around her lower jaw, held in place by her lower teeth. She looked like a golden-retriever mix. She seemed the more amenable of the two dogs. I held on to her, moving with them and talking to them, trying to calm them down. "It's okay. It's okay. Take it easy, Punkins. Take it easy. We can fix this."

The dogs' heads needed to be close to one another in order for the collar to be loosened enough to go over the golden's long bottom teeth. Someone behind me said, "That one you're holdin' onto is Bailey. Her people are at work. She comes over and stays in my yard so Chop can keep her company. They always loved each other. Nothing like this ever happened before. What's wrong with them?"

"Come over here and see if you can hold Chop's head still. The dogs are okay. See how the collar is wrapped around Bailey's jaw? We need to get it off. Chop is more freaked out than she is."

"We were afraid to get too close to 'em in case they were sick or gone crazy. Damn. I see."

Chop's owner took hold of his dog's head. He tried to hold his panicky dog still but neither of us was able to keep the dogs from continuing to struggle and twist. They wanted to pull away from one another, but we needed to get them closer and calmer to fix the problem. Bailey was getting worn out. She was the dog more likely to be injured, and she seemed to be slowing down, but Chop's adrenaline kept him fighting and whipping his head and body back and forth. His eyes were wide. He wanted to fight and bite and I didn't want him to bite me—or anyone else.

We had to get Chop's mouth closed. He was too strong and determined to let his owner hold his jaw, so his muzzle needed to be tied. I thought the dog's owner would have more luck getting his dog calmed enough to submit to a muzzle wrap. We were lucky that Chop had a nice shepherd kind of nose rather than a bull-doggy nose.

"Wrap the leash around his muzzle twice and tie it behind his ears. Then we can maneuver him more easily."

After a few tries, Chop's owner managed a good safe wrap. Another neighbor came over to help lift the dog off the ground. The two men held him steady enough that I could move Bailey to a position where I could get the chain over her lower teeth and off. Never was there a happier, more grateful dog. Except maybe for Chop, after his teeth were set free. The bystanders cheered, the dogs bounced around the yard. A problem solved. I loved my job.

My all-time favorite hero episode happened late one afternoon when I received a call to assist the police who were entering an unoccupied house to execute a search warrant. Although no humans were in the house, the officers had been surprised by the dogs. Normally they knew if there would be dogs in a target house and called Animal Control in advance to meet them. Usually two or more AC officers were dispatched to handle these kinds of calls. One officer would roll a big garbage can in the door to fend off the dog(s) while another officer or officers would capture the dog(s) with a "come-along" stick—a metal pole with a retractable noose. The process was tricky, but it was effective. I only heard about one time when reinforcements had to be called in to sedate an animal before a warrant could be executed. Reinforcements were from the Department of Fish and

Game. Their techniques were usually needed for mountain lions or bears that were too close to residential areas, but they helped Animal Control with other problems involving wild animals or dangerous domestic animals. They provided traps we used for troublesome urban raccoons, coyotes, skunks, opossums and foxes, all of whom adapted well to city life.

The dogs at this house were a big surprise to the police officers. They fully expected the premises to be empty. I was assigned the call because I was the nearest field officer. The other field officers were in different quarters of the city, at least 30 minutes or more away. I arrived at the house within ten minutes of receiving the emergency call. Four police officers were on the sidewalk outside the chain link fence that surrounded the property. Two officers were the ones originally detailed to execute the search warrant and the other two arrived as backup after they heard over the radio that there was a problem at the address.

The original officers had keys to the house. This was supposed to be a simple search of an unoccupied residence. The people who lived there did not own dogs. However, after the officers opened the front door, dogs came running and barking from somewhere at the back of the house. The two men barely managed to slam the screen door behind them as they ran back down the walk and out the front gate. All four officers took out their weapons when I insisted on going up to the door to see what we would be dealing with. I imagine they planned to shoot the dogs, not me, but I was between them and the dogs as I walked up to the house. None of the officers offered to go with me.

I walked up three steps to the small cement front porch. The front door was at right angles to the porch. I saw two beautiful Dobermans on the other side of the screen. They started barking as I walked toward the porch, and they barked louder when I was close enough to see them, but they didn't lunge at the screen door. They were sleek, with show-cropped ears, and they looked like they were barking with excitement rather than malice. Both were wearing collars—one red and one blue—with tags attached.

Ordinarily, protective or vicious dogs would be trying their best to destroy any barrier between them and whatever they thought of as the enemy. That would be me, but I didn't seem to be a serious threat to them. On a hunch I said loudly, "Sit!" and gave the hand signal to sit. Both dogs immediately stopped barking and sat. They remained in place when I opened the screen a little. I opened it a little more, put leashes over their heads, and walked them down to the front gate. None of the officers moved to open the gate for us. They stared at the dogs, while keeping a respectful distance. I opened the gate and took the dogs to my truck, where I lifted them into cages—still with no help from the police, who were busy putting their weapons away. The backup officers got into their patrol car and drove away. The other two officers nodded and said "thank you" before getting on with executing their search warrant. I filled out my paperwork and drove away with the friendly Dobermans. I did not expect a thank you card this time, but I felt like a superhero anyway and grinned all the way back to the shelter.

CHAPTER 18

BRAN FLAKES

More than two years after gaining the unofficial title of Animal Control's designated snake handler because of my accidental success with "Kitty" the python, I received my second snake call. The dispatcher remembered my snake handler designation and gave the job to me. This time a realtor called because a repair man, hired to fix the dryer in a condominium she had listed, had fled the job. He ran down the stairs from the third floor in about 10 seconds according to residents who were witnesses. He was screaming "SNAKE! THERE'S A SNAKE! A SNAKE!" and he drove away in his van. The realtor verified with the appliance repair company that the repair man was not planning to come back. In fact, he was taking some time off. The repair company declined to send another representative until the snake was confirmed to have been removed from the premises.

No description for the snake or its specific location was available. Presumably it was located somewhere in the vicinity of the dryer in the condo. As the designated snake handler, I was delighted to respond to the call. When I arrived at the building, the realtor took me up to the third-floor, unlocked the door of the empty condo and said, "Let me know when you're finished." She left after handing me her card. My assumption was that this snake was another lost or abandoned pet, and more than likely not dangerous, but I proceeded with caution.

The dryer was pulled out from its closet into a narrow hallway. I noticed an abandoned tool box on top of the washing machine. The most likely place for the repair man to have encountered the snake was in or around the dryer. Gingerly, I opened the door of the dryer. No snake, but the drum was slightly off kilter. The alleged snake didn't show itself as I looked around the area near the dryer. I thought it possible that the screaming repair man had scared it into slithering away. It could be anywhere. It could be a dead snake. Given his reaction, the repair man probably didn't look at it long enough to verify if it was dead or alive.

The back panel of the dryer had been removed. To access the area where the animal was probably last seen, I had to climb over the dryer and squeeze into the space between the dryer and the wall. Small metal pieces, screws and washers were all over the floor. The drum looked as if it was in the process of being removed when the repair work stopped. If a snake happened to be in there, I didn't want to squash it or injure it, so I poked around carefully, wearing my thick leather gloves just in case. I tried to lift the drum a little.

There it was. A snake. A small snake, and he was alive. Having done a little homework on snakes after meeting the first one, I knew this one for a boa constrictor—not poisonous. I removed my gloves. A boa is capable of biting but not likely to do so, the same as Kitty the python. My previous success with Kitty gave me courage. I wasn't planning to bother him any more than was necessary to free him from his predicament. If I could free him without inflicting further damage, he would most likely remain unprovoked, I hoped. The drum had been keeping him pinned, but he was still trying to move a little. He was too worn out to move much on his own. With some careful maneuvering of the drum, the snake managed to wiggle free. He was moving too slowly to get away from me and once I was able to grasp the back of his head, he managed to wrap himself around my forearm. Another grateful, friendly snake.

This reptile was a small brown boa, less than two feet long. His scales were roughed up in a couple of places and he was lethargic. I asked the dispatcher to locate a veterinarian in the area that treated reptiles. The closest reptile vet was only five minutes away, and we—the snake and I—went there directly while the dispatcher called the realtor to let her know the problem had been cleared.

The vet recognized the disheveled snake. He showed me a flyer from its owner with a picture confirming that we had the advertised snake, named Bran Flakes, which had disappeared from a fourth-floor condominium in the building where it was found. Bran Flakes had been missing for almost a month. The veterinarian said he thought the snake could be treated and recover from the damage to its scales, but scale damage could be a serious problem. He wanted to keep the patient for a few days of observation. While I was in the vet's office, he called Bran Flakes' owner to let him know that his snake had been found. The owner agreed to be financially responsible for his pet's care, and I went on to my next assignment.

About two weeks later, I visited the veterinarian who had taken Bran Flakes to ask how the snake was doing. He said that the little snake might need further treatment if his skin didn't shed properly. The owner reported that the snake ate a thawed mouse a day after he was released from care, a very good sign. Prognosis excellent for complete recovery. I was glad to know that Bran Flakes was doing well, not so happy to hear about his meal. I know what snakes eat, but I prefer to think of them as vegetarians.

CHAPTER 19

HAL

The last three snake calls that I handled were all for the same snake. The first time I met the almost seven-foot-long Burmese python, was on a chilly but sunny November afternoon, when a man doing work in his back yard found the snake curled up sunning itself on a stack of cardboard. "Enough to give ya' a heart attack. Still not sure I'm not gonna have one." The homeowner pointed into his large back yard where his riding lawnmower stood near something that looked like a pile of leaves, on top of some flattened cardboard boxes. In November fallen leaves were long gone. Moving closer, I saw that the snake's markings looked more like dark puzzle pieces on a gold background.

By the time I encountered this snake, I knew enough about them to recognize this one as a Burmese python, known to be docile and popular as pets. Burmese pythons are the ones that have invaded the Florida Everglades, thanks to discarded or escaped pets. They can grow up to 18-feet long. This one was lethargic and sleepily friendly. Burmese pythons don't do well in cold weather. He had been looking for a bit of warmth on a cool day, and was happy to let me drape him around me like a shawl. He was too big to contain in a portable cage. Animal Control trucks were never meant to transport snakes.

I helped this slow-moving reptile to wrap his tail around my left arm. He was willing. His head wound around my right arm. He was easier to carry when he held on. I worried that his health might be at risk in the cold air. His species lives naturally in warm climates. Wearing him back to the shelter while he enjoyed the warmth in the cab of my truck, I wondered if any other drivers noticed my passenger. A dog-catcher wearing a big snake is not something seen every day.

Later that day a woman came to the shelter to claim the snake, who she said was named Hal. She said Hal had been abandoned by her former boyfriend and she was planning to sell it. The girl wasn't fond of snakes. She couldn't bring herself to touch him, but she thought she could get some money for Hal. He was large and he was beautiful. She remained at a distance as I helped the young man who accompanied her load Hal into a canvas bag. The girl promised to make sure Hal was secured in his terrarium. No charge for Animal Control's services.

A couple of weeks later, another call came in. "There's a snake stuck in a motorcycle." This time, Hal had crawled up under the back fenders of a Vespa motor scooter and had wrapped himself around the still-warm motor. He was again searching for a place to get warm. Neighbors saw the snake disappear into the scooter, amazed that the whole animal fit into such a small space. Nothing indicated that anything strange was happening in the scooter by looking at it. The snake was completely concealed. If the witnesses had not been there, the scooter's owner would have been in for a shocking surprise.

From the witnesses' description of the snake, I was certain that it was Hal. We were in Hal's neighborhood. The only way to get him out of his hiding place was to remove the scooter's fenders. Someone notified the owner of the Vespa, who showed up about 10 minutes after I arrived, while I was discussing with my dispatcher the possibility of having the scooter impounded. The owner said he had the tools to remove the fenders but he was not interested in doing the job. I asked him to get the tools and stand by to give me what instructions he could.

A crowd of onlookers gathered during the hour-long project. Hal was wrapped snugly around the motor. Unwrapping him was like untangling a rope. He had knotted himself in place. I had to run his head back through loops to free him. He didn't seem to mind the untangling process. I wondered if he was laughing to himself as all this was going on. Snakes aren't normally associated with a sense of humor, but it's possible. Bystanders offered suggestions as they enjoyed the afternoon's unusual entertainment.

I enjoyed wearing Hal back to the shelter again. This time we knew who to call to pick him up and this time the shelter supervisor charged the girl $20.00 for our services, as an incentive to keep the snake at home. The fee was entirely arbitrary, since no laws covered stray pet snakes.

The $20.00 wasn't enough. A few days later, I picked Hal up from a garden shed. I think he was glad to see me. I took him to his home this time, hoping the girl, whose name was Nancy, would surrender him. Nancy still could not bring herself to touch him. She refused to take him from me, but she said she wanted to keep "it." She hadn't done anything to advertise him for sale, but she still thought she would be able to get some big bucks for Hal. I attempted to hand him over, knowing she wouldn't be able to take him, and I declined to go inside her apartment to place him in the insecure terrarium from which he had already escaped three times. She said she would go call a friend who would take him from me for her. The only thing I could think of to discourage her from taking him back was to threaten to issue a ticket for a leash law violation. The neighbors wanted the snake out of the neighborhood, but none of the laws I was charged with enforcing fit the crime. If she agreed to accept the citation, the worst that could happen was that the ticket would be thrown out by a judge if she contested it.

A leash law violation carried an $80.00 fine for a first offense. I thought the threat of an $80.00 fine might make Nancy see reason.

"If you want to keep him, you have to take responsibility for him. I'm not waiting here for someone else to come and take custody of your snake. Either surrender him or accept the citation and pay the $80.00 fine."

The threat of the fine or the fear of having to touch the snake caused her to make the right choice. She surrendered him, signing a release form. Hal's next stop was the zoo. After a vet-check and a period of quarantine, the zoo found Hal a safe, secure home where he was appreciated.

My snake handling days ended with Hal. Since the day I wore him to the zoo, I have never been close to another snake. They can be stunningly beautiful, but they are not warm and fuzzy and they are not vegetarians. Confining them in terrariums seems unkind, though there are plenty of arguments against my way of thinking. I don't know that any of the three snakes I met on the job appreciated my efforts on their behalf. They didn't bite me. I take that as a positive sign we were getting along. I don't know. Dogs and cats are easier to read. I'm glad I met those three lovely snakes, and I hope they all lived happily.

CHAPTER 20

BERT AND CARL

Seattle Animal Control had about fifteen field officers when I went to work there in 1980. Might have been more—or less. Most of them were characters I'd like to see in a book—loveable, unique, drawn outside the lines—or in just one case, dislikeable and unique. Two of my favorite working partners were Bert and Carl. Bert was a big gruff ex-Marine, a hero in the Korean war with a pile of medals—"Not worth much now. Not worth talkin' about. I don't even like to look at 'em," was his comment when I asked about the medals. His half-Korean daughter told us that he had been a big hero. She told us about his medals, but not even she knew the stories associated with them.

Bert always looked a little wrinkled, a little sleepy. His grizzled gray hair was usually too long. His nose was crooked from an old football injury and red—from sunburn, not alcohol. When I worked with him—sometimes we were sent out in pairs for certain calls or when one of the trucks was out of service—as we drove around the city we mostly talked about food. He didn't like to talk about himself but he loved to talk about food and cooking. Sometimes he talked about his four black toy poodles. He loved those poodles. He made gourmet dog treats for them, which he carried in his pockets most of the time.

Many dogs are wary of large men. When we were on patrol, we picked up strays if complaints came in from certain neighborhoods. Bert hunkered down and spoke softly to scared or suspicious animals on the street, doling out treats when necessary. Women officers were mostly better than the men at rounding up strays, but Bert's treats gave him an edge over the rest of the guys.

Bert assured me that his feelings weren't hurt when I managed to corral a dog that he couldn't get close to, but I think he felt a little bad. He loved dogs as much as I did. When he was home, his poodles always gravitated to him. His wife and daughter were second on the poodles' list of preferences. His daughter said it was comical the way the dogs insisted on piling onto the big man when he was in his favorite chair. They wouldn't move for anything except dinner, and he did his best not to disturb them.

If the dogs we picked up on patrol had tags, we took them home. Otherwise they usually went to the shelter. Because people had only three days to claim their pets, we made every effort to find owners of strays we picked up. Bert was particularly conscientious about trying to find owners. He would knock on doors in neighborhoods where I didn't like to get out of the truck. Too many people thought of us as wicked characters who chased defenseless puppies for no good reason. Our reasons, of course, had to do with complaints by members of the public and the city statutes relating to animals. I had a few bad experiences knocking on doors. I don't like people I don't know to yell at me for no good reason. Bert didn't mind. He sometimes found owners of dogs or someone who knew the owner, and he left his card with friendly locals to give the dogs their best chance of getting back home.

Although I was good at catching dogs, I told Bert that I was a terrible cook and I never had anything good to take to potlucks. He wrote out a detailed—and I mean microscopically detailed—recipe for Quiche Lorraine for me. "Try it, girl. Ya won't miss." He was right. I followed his directions to the letter and made the most impressive quiche I've ever seen (or eaten). The made-from-scratch crust was golden-brown, flaky and almost painfully delicious. The filling made people gasp with pleasure and disbelief. No one believed I made it until I produced it a few times with witnesses. I had to give Bert the credit. My friends knew that I couldn't cook.

That quiche was the only fabulous food I ever made (to this day) and for a few short years, I fed it to my friends over and over. I lost the handwritten instructions during a move. Bert was out of my life by that time. Trying to make the quiche from memory failed miserably. Some of my old friends still mention my Quiche Lorraine potluck days nostalgically. I still give Bert the credit, as I hand over my potluck offering of store-bought cookies or chips and pre-packaged dip.

Another character who partnered with me occasionally was Carl. He wasn't allowed to drive the trucks we took out on calls because he had a prosthetic left leg, which was deemed a liability issue, even though he was capable of driving. He was also frequently high, but neither his hand-made leg nor his drug-altered states interfered with his ability to do the job, usually that of dispatcher. The supervisors let him slide by. He was good at his job. He was also just plain likeable. His wicked sense of humor made riding with him entertaining and fun.

Ordinarily Carl spent his shifts at the dispatch desk, but once in a while he went out in the world. Officers with minor injuries were assigned to dispatch if they weren't able to work safely in the field and Carl rode shotgun with one or another of the field officers when he was bumped from the dispatch desk. He always made himself useful.

Carl came with me on one assignment I won't ever forget. We went to pick up a wild cat trapped in someone's bedroom. That kind of call wasn't unusual. Wild cats turned up in unlikely places. Sometimes they weren't wild. They were antisocial, which amounted to the same thing in terms of behavior. The apartment that was our destination was the converted attic of a large three-story house, and access required walking up an old wooden staircase built at the side of the house. We climbed slowly up to the little landing outside the apartment door, with Carl dragging his leg up each step. He refused to wait in the truck.

Catching the cat didn't take long. Carl and I were both well-practiced at rounding up unwilling cats in confined spaces. The cat flailed and screeched with its neck in the noose at the end of the come-along stick, as wild cats do. Normally we would go outside and immediately put the cat in a small portable cage, but outside this door, the small porch platform was maybe four feet by five feet, and the railing and supports around it wouldn't have confined a frantic cat if anything went wrong. We didn't want the cat to fall three stories, nor did we want to put ourselves in danger. Caging or bagging the cat indoors was out of the question.

I held the stick with the traumatized cat at the other end. Carl went outside first. I didn't expect his help getting down the stairs. I followed him, trying to steady the cat and not succeeding very well. This cat was wild, filled with adrenaline and not small. At the door I turned my head briefly to take leave of the apartment owner. When I turned back, feeling a little sick about having to take on the miserable job of grappling the poor cat down the stairs, Carl was leaning against the railing at the top of the stairs with a big grin on his face. "Aren't you glad I'm not somebody else? I'd be real unhappy with you." The cat was firmly attached to his artificial left leg slightly above his knee, with its teeth and all four sets of claws dug in deep. At that moment I was unbelievably glad he was the guy with the fake leg. Cats can inflict serious injuries. Cat scratch fever had put one of the field officers in the hospital not long before this incident.

I wasn't sure if I should laugh or apologize or both. Carl took the stick from me and secured it to his heavy-duty police utility belt without disturbing his passenger. (We wore the belts to carry two-way radios and long, heavy black flashlights.) The cat stayed put. Then Carl used the handrails on either side of the steps to swing himself down the stairs, three at a time. By the time I got to the bottom, he had caged the cat and put it in the truck.

Animal Control drew in an assortment of curious characters, possibly including me. Another of my co-workers said that I was the strangest person he ever met, but I don't think he had a wide circle of acquaintances. I didn't like him well enough to give him much credence and I didn't mind being in Animal Control's cast of characters. He was the unlikeable guy. He was out of place. He was the guy whose back pockets were always torn because he couldn't seem to absorb the important rules—*Never turn your back on an angry dog and never, ever run away*. He didn't last long—couldn't afford to keep replacing his uniform pants.

CHAPTER 21

FRANKY

I wish I could have saved all of them, but only a tiny percentage of the worthy animals that came through the shelter managed to make it to my personal, unsanctioned foster program. A few animals came to my house to stay forever, but five dogs, three cats and a parrot was my limit for permanent residency. Exceptional animals that weren't officially adoptable or that hadn't been adopted within the three-day period deserved to have good homes, and some of us worked outside official channels to see that they were placed with responsible owners. On one extraordinary day I navigated an especially difficult maze to find the perfect home for a Shar-Pei called Franky.

Franky was black with inch-long hair that grew straight out from his wrinkled body. Petting him was like petting an expensive plush carpet. He was a beautiful example of his breed. Shar-Pei's were bred as farm dogs and later as fighting dogs. They are like a Chinese version of a pit bull in some ways. They have strong jaws and the ability to put up a good fight if necessary. Their wrinkles protect the dogs from injuries to vulnerable parts of the body. They are described as affectionate and devoted pets, but "often stand-offish with strangers" in the American Kennel Club (AKC) breed standard. They are protective of their people and their territory.

Franky came from Oregon to Seattle where he was left at the Seattle Animal Control shelter near the end of business hours. The man who brought him in said he was a friend of the owner. He said that the owner lived in Oregon and was unable to keep the dog, Franky, for reasons unknown. "But this is a real nice dog, cost a lot of money. He deserves a good home," the man said as he scribbled through the surrender paperwork and all but ran out the door. The owner's friend left the paperwork with the $5.00 surrender fee, but he left most of the page blank. We had no information about the man who abandoned the dog or about the former owner from Oregon. We suspected they might be one and the same.

The only useful information given on the intake form about Franky was a short note that said, "He's not that great with small children." The shelter supervisor felt there was a good chance that the dog had bitten someone, since he had been transported all the way from Oregon. He was a quality example of his breed. Why dump him at a city shelter? The person who anonymously left him indicated he had a "not that great" attitude toward small children. All of the information we had indicated that Franky had some kind of shady past. If we had information that the dog was not good with children, no matter what other qualities he had, he became unsuitable for adoption.

The Shar-Pei was gentle and friendly with everyone working at the shelter. He seemed to have an abnormally friendly temperament for the breed. Children who came into the shelter area were greeted by the same friendly wag as everyone else who approached the kennel run where Franky was confined. No one was supposed to approach him. He was confined in a quarantine area at the back of the kennel room, but the quarantine kennels were separated from the rest of the kennels by a single heavy chain with a sign in the center that said "NO TRESPASSING" in big red letters.

The temporary warehouse facility didn't have a separate room for quarantining dogs. The law required a ten-day quarantine for rabies for dogs with a confirmed or suspected bite in their immediate history. Most of the biters were euthanized when their ten days ended. Sometimes first offenders were taken home if the dog had a normally gentle temperament and the owners promised to keep it confined. The arbitrary ten-day period didn't take into account that rabies can have a much longer incubation period, but the law was the law. The only way to actually confirm a rabies diagnosis was by autopsy. If a dog had two documented bites, that meant a death sentence after the quarantine period, unless a court intervened.

Some dog-owners tried to prevent execution of their dogs by taking the issue to court. Those dogs stayed incarcerated until the court decided their fate. Most dogs that bite are not vicious. In fact, most dogs will bite if conditions are right. A dog might overly be protective of food or of a toy. A startled dog might bite as a reflex. "Let sleeping dogs lie" is a good idea. At least be wary of sleeping dogs, especially old ones with a hearing deficit. Dogs that are badly hurt will almost always try to bite in an attempt to protect themselves. Some people were desperate to save beloved pets and their dogs stayed in the quarantine kennels for months, until the courts got around to deciding the dog's fate.

Franky caused people to ignore the "NO TRESPASSING" sign. If some people caught sight of that wrinkled, grinning Shar-Pei face, they went over or under the chain to get a closer look. Franky was so unusual and appealing that they couldn't help themselves. He was always welcoming, and he never barked—not at loud noises or screaming children or even in response to other dogs barking. Many people asked to adopt him, but his fate had been decided by that note on his intake paperwork. We put him in the farthest kennel away from the chain barrier, but his head could still be seen through the chain link from certain angles. A conspiracy of kennel attendants and field officers decided that the dog called Franky should not die and that he should go home with me when his quarantine ended. My house had the most secure accommodations for dogs, thanks to Robert Reddog, my escape-artist pit bull.

Most of the kennel staff could not agree with the shelter supervisor's decision, correct though it was under the circumstances, to euthanize the Shar-Pei after a quarantine period. We didn't know if he really had bitten someone. He could have been euthanized the day he came in if the shelter manager decided he wasn't adoptable, but he was given a 10-day reprieve under the guise of a quarantine period. Everybody was charmed by his looks and by his grin. After getting to know Franky, we couldn't let him die on speculation about his past. His temperament was better than or equal to most of the dogs put up for adoption. "Not good with small children," could mean almost any dog under certain circumstances, and there was no evidence that he actually bit anyone. He may have been too energetic to play with small children. In my opinion, irresponsible or ignorant parents cause more dog-related injuries of small children than do either the dogs or the children involved. Franky was exuberant, playful and strong. Any dog of his size and temperament should be carefully supervised around small children.

We smuggled him out to my custody when his ten days

were up. Franky came to my house to be fostered. He got along well with all five of my dogs, including my pit bull, Robert. I began the task of finding him the perfect home. The Shar-Pei breed is known for having some health issues, although Franky didn't show any signs of the common eye or skin problems. He also carried the stigma of having been labeled "not that great with small children." His pool of perfect pet owners was limited. I expected to foster him for at least several weeks, maybe months, before finding him the right home.

Four days after he came to stay with me, I decided to take Franky with me to a friend's house, where I was feeding cats and watering plants while my friend was away. The weather forecast called for snow later in the day, but when I left my house, I was sure I had plenty of time before the snowfall. The temperature was close to freezing but the sun was shining. I thought the report of snow was probably wrong anyway. Reports of snow, more often than not, resulted in the familiar Seattle rain. Before I had driven the seven miles to my friend's house, gray clouds spread over the sky and snow began to fall.

I needed to be quick about completing my house-sitting duties and decided to get gas on my way home instead of stopping beforehand. The gas gauge was on empty, but there was a Chevron nearby, on the right side of the street in the direction of home. I figured I could make it that far after a quick feeding and watering.

By the time I had driven down the long driveway to my friend's house and had parked the car, powdery snow was beginning to stick to the ground. I was a little nervous and distracted at the notion of driving all the way back home in the snow. Franky took advantage of my distraction when I stepped out of the car onto the snow-dusted gravel. He jumped over the front seat and hopped out of the car behind me. He ran past me, back down the long driveway, leaving paw prints in the snow. I could do nothing but follow his tracks. My tennis shoes were not good for running in snow (or walking for that matter) but his prints were clear, so I followed. When I had tracked him about a quarter of a mile to the end of the long block, his paw-prints disappeared into the slush of a busy four-lane cross-street. I trudged back to my car, thinking about my stupidity and about all the bad things that could happen to a dog running loose through busy city streets in snow.

When I finally made it back to my car, cold and wet, there was Franky sitting next to the driver's door, impatiently waiting for me to let him back in. He was almost as cold and wet as I was. I have no idea how he got back to the car without my seeing him. By the time I found him sitting by the car, any prints he left had been covered by falling flakes that were coming thicker and faster.

After tending the cats and plants, our next destination was to be the gas station, which was less than a mile away. When we reached the station, a big sign reading "Closed due to snow" let me know I should have stopped for gas on the way, not on the way back. Already cars were sliding down the hill in front of the gas station toward the freeway entrance. My good old '69 Volvo made it to the freeway entrance without incident. A Texaco station was at the next exit, less than half a mile down the freeway, so I turned onto I-5 South and ran out of gas about 50 feet past the ramp. My tennis shoes were soaked from following the run-away dog, and the rest of me was the same. The only option, if I didn't want to freeze in place, was to get out of the car and walk to the next exit. Cell phones had not arrived to save us all from such mishaps.

Fortunately, a city water truck stopped to give me a ride before I had slogged far. The driver dropped me off at the next exit ramp. I walked up the ramp and across a four-lane street to get to the gas station. The distance seemed much longer in the snow than I remembered it. The station attendant loaned me a gas can and filled it with a gallon of gas. I set off on foot again through almost two inches of snow. I wasn't wearing a hat. A hat seemed unnecessary. At least there were mittens in the glove compartment. I must have looked as miserable and bedraggled as I felt, with my mittens dripping icicles onto the gas can and my hair dripping icicles onto my shoulders. Another good Samaritan stopped to give me a ride back to my car while I was walking down the ramp on the other side of the freeway from the gas station. The driver said with a grin, "I won't ask. Just tell me where you're headed."

After he dropped me off and helped me get my car gassed up and started, I drove to the gas station to return the can and finish filling up the tank. That done, I attempted to head out the driveway exit that would have taken me back to the freeway. My car slid backwards down the shallow incline. My only other choice was an exit that sent me in the opposite direction from where I wanted to go. I exited onto the other street, heading south, away from the freeway and away from home. Within less than a minute a pickup truck backed out of a driveway directly in front of me. My car was going about 15 miles per hour, but he was so close that I would have broadsided him if I hadn't braked. The truck took off while my car fishtailed and slid slowly across the street where it came to rest against the side of the front bumper of an older model parked car. The owner of the car happened to be standing on the other side of it removing snow from his windshield. I was getting out of my car when he said, "Don't worry about it. It's just another dimple." He came around his car and with one hand he pushed my car backward off his bumper. The car continued sliding without me in it. The door hung open, an invitation for Franky to make another run, which spurred me to try to catch the car. As I tried to get back into the moving car, the door knocked me down. The back of my head hit the snow-covered pavement and my car continued backing in a wide curve down the street, into the side of another car that was parked in front of an office building.

My head was sore, but Franky had stayed in the back seat. I left him there in the warm car while I went into the office building looking for the owner of the damaged car. She took my insurance information. She was pleasant about it all. She must have felt sorry for me. I would have felt sorry for me. When I got back in the car, I realized I was about two blocks from my doctor's office. My head hurt. Maybe I should have it checked out. If the doctor wasn't there, I could park in his parking lot and rest from the morning's ordeal. My Volvo didn't want to drive in the snow any more than I did. Her front bumper was sorely wounded.

The small parking lot outside the doctor's office had only one car in it, Dr. Nelson's Audi. He was in his office. All his appointments for the rest of the day had cancelled. He examined my head while I told him about my terrible, horrible, no good day. He wanted me to stay in the office for a while with ice on the back of my head, and he invited Franky inside to stay with me.

Dr. Nelson was fascinated with Franky. The doctor was an animal person. He lived outside of the city and had two dogs, some cats, a ferret, a couple of horses and some teenagers. He and Franky bonded while I iced my head, dried my hair and shoes and warmed up the rest of me. Franky had found his forever-home.

The next time I saw Dr. Nelson, a few weeks later, the doctor told me how happy his family was to have the Shar-Pei. They re-named him Frun Ki in honor of his Chinese heritage. Frun Ki did something that Dr. Nelson particularly appreciated. The dog showed off his Shar-Pei temperament by protecting the doctor's fifteen-year-old daughter, Cherie. She brought home her new boyfriend who was going to have dinner with the family. The two teens were in the kitchen, helping to get things ready for dinner when the boyfriend attempted to put his arm around Cherie and Frun Ki thought it was way too soon for that sort of thing. The doctor thought so too. The dog took hold of the boy's back pocket, pulling him away from Cherie. Only the pocket received minor damage.

The rest of the evening, Frun Ki was friendly, as long as the boy kept a respectful distance from Cherie. The doctor said he wanted to send the dog on all of their subsequent dates, but Cherie wasn't good with that. After that incident, despite his good work, Frun Ki was banished to the basement when guests came over, unless the guests had been pre-approved by the dog. Franky/Frun Ki was a most successful placement done in record time.

CHAPTER 22

A MONKEY

The public used to have a fixed stereotype for Animal Control Officers. We were still associated with the cartoon versions of the evil dogcatcher wielding a net to catch stray animals. We didn't usually wield a net (unless we were trying to catch ducklings on the freeway) but we did catch stray dogs or give citations to people who let their dogs run loose. Sometimes we trapped stray cats. We also did a variety of lesser-known and more interesting things. Once I was sent to pick up a monkey.

One night at about 9:00 pm our Animal Control dispatcher received a call from the police for an assist in a wooded area of West Seattle. I was the only field officer on duty that evening. A West Seattle resident had been arrested for discharging a firearm and I needed to pick up his pets, one of which was a monkey.

The location was an area hidden from the main road, where people had built small houses on either side of a deep ravine. Many of the houses were supported by long posts at the front because of the steep angle of incline, and several of the homes looked like do-it-yourself projects. The access road was at the bottom of the ravine, unpaved and one lane wide. The house that was my destination had a long—maybe 75 steps—rickety wooden staircase up to the front door. The posts supporting the front of the house looked solid, and the little house itself, although covered in different shades of white paint, looked as though it had been constructed by someone who took care to make the angles square and walls solid. The house had a peaked, shingled roof, while several of the other homes had flat metal roofs, placing some of them more in the category of shacks. The stairs up to the house didn't look quite as reliably solid as the house itself.

The police had the home-owner—an elderly, inebriated, former merchant seaman—and his rifle in custody. A police officer told me that I was to pick up a parrot and a monkey in the house. A dog had already been taken in by a neighbor. The monkey was chained in the living room. The other piece of information given to me by the officer was that the monkey was accustomed to drinking a beer a day. The old man insisted that I be informed about the beer a day.

I had originally assumed the monkey was probably a spider monkey or some other small primate. People sometimes kept those as pets, but when I climbed the 75 steps and went into the little house at the top, I found a fat, female yellow baboon, almost four feet tall with a heavy metal collar and a chain attached to a ring in the floor. She looked scared, her facial expression similar to a human's. She showed her big teeth with a submissive smile, and her eyes were open wide in fear. She backed up to the wall across the tiny room, as far as her chain allowed. She didn't appear to be aggressive, but any frightened animal is potentially dangerous. Her chain would have kept her from being able to reach me, even with her long arms. She didn't move toward me, though. When I moved closer, she tried to pull farther back. Her yellow hair was dirty and straggly, and she didn't appear to be young. A shallow crater in the wooden floor indicated she had been chained for a long time. She must have been a baby when she was smuggled into this country. From what I knew of wild animal smugglers and poachers, they didn't usually bother with adult animals.

One of the police officers stuck his head in the door about 10 minutes after I entered the house to see how I was getting along with the baboon. He shook his head, came inside and picked up the squawking, swearing parrot in its cage. "Another neighbor said he'd take this until the guy gets back home, but the monkey isn't legal. We—you have to get it out of here and take it to the zoo or someplace. How long you think that might be?"

"I have no idea. Could be quite a while. Would you make sure nobody else comes up here? She needs to calm down." I sat on the radiator near the door because the only chair was on the other side of the room, too close to the big monkey. I talked to her for about forty-five minutes before I showed her the four-foot-long metal stick with a noose at the end that I was going to have to use to take her down the steps. Among the things I told her was that monkey bites were extremely dangerous because of the bacteria in monkey's mouths—similar to humans. I kept talking—about anything that came to mind—until she relaxed a little.

When I showed her the stick, we played with it for a while. I showed her how it worked by putting the noose over my head. Eventually she put the noose over her head a few times, and eventually I tightened it against her metal collar. I was able to unclip the chain from the floor. From there, the two of us moved a foot or two at a time toward the steps, then down the steps, one careful step at a time. I kept talking, and she seemed to be listening. From first contact until we were down the steps to my truck took more than two hours. We were almost friends.

I thought that getting her into the cage at the back of the truck would be difficult, but after I opened the door, she hopped up on her own. When I loosened the noose, she lifted it over her head. She didn't seem bothered by my closing the cage door.

The dispatcher radioed Al, the night-zookeeper at the Woodland Park Zoo to let him know I would be bringing him a guest, a baboon, but the dispatcher went off shift after he talked to Al. Three hours later, when I radioed Al to let him know I was on the way, he had almost given up on us. He was excited to be receiving a beer-drinking baboon. When I drove into the zoo enclosure, he had refreshments waiting for both of us. The baboon enjoyed a bowl of fruit and vegetables while he and I ate cookies and watched her. She settled into her new temporary home, a quarantine enclosure. Al said he would find her some toys. He invited me to come back at the end of her six-week quarantine to see how she was doing.

At the end of the six weeks, I went back to the zoo after my shift ended, and Al let me see my monkey friend. She was still in the quarantine cage, sitting on a bench with an empty beer can at her feet. I peeked at her through a tiny window. She couldn't see me. She had been bathed and groomed, and her big beer belly was even more noticeable. Al said that she was still drinking a beer a day, and she was being treated for parasites. A permanent home had been arranged for her at a zoo in Houston, Texas, which had facilities for taking care of geriatric primates. The keepers and medical staff in Houston would decide whether or not to wean her off her daily brew.

I never knew what happened to the man who had kept the monkey for so long. I wondered how long she had been chained in that room. She must have been around other humans besides her owner, because even though she was afraid of me at first, we didn't have much difficulty becoming acquainted. She would have been good company, but chaining her like that was a crime of cruelty. The man wasn't charged. Losing her was probably punishment enough. Having her so close to me, seeing her expressions made it clear to me—like nothing in a textbook ever did—that she wasn't far removed from our species. Meeting her was a highlight in my life, a privilege. No wonder I loved my job.

CHAPTER 23

JANET AND RUPERT

Janet lived in a park downhill from an affluent neighborhood near the University of Washington. She had a big, beautiful German Shepard named Louise. Janet appeared to be in her late fifties or early sixties. She may have been younger. Life on the street—or in the park—doesn't usually allow people to age well. However, she was almost always reasonably well-groomed, and I saw her in several different dresses, all light, summery knee-length dresses that she could slip over her head, which she did from time to time, revealing a lack of undergarments. She had a supply of blankets somewhere back in the trees, and sometimes when the weather was cold, she wrapped herself and Louise in one of them. I knew she had more than one because they were all brightly colored—red, blue, yellow, green—at least one of each. Her belongings were somewhere among the evergreen trees and bushes in the part of the park that backed up to a steep hill.

In the summer when I waved to her, Janet waved back, but if I got out of my truck she and Louise ran toward the bushes. I learned to stay in my truck unless I was on a call to pick up Louise. I never had a real conversation with Janet, but she seemed to recognize me and she was friendly from a distance, even though the times we had closer contact weren't pleasant for her. I had to impound

Louise several times. Those were the times she was in police custody and usually screaming for help. "Don't do it. Please don't! H-e-e-lp! Don't take her!" After a few of the most hysterical episodes attempting to restrain Janet, the police learned that if they waited until Animal Control (often me) took Louise away, Janet settled down, maybe because she knew her dog was safe. Still, she yelled all the while I was leading Louise to my truck, but when the dog had been loaded up, Janet quit resisting the officers. If she wasn't allowed to see Louise put into the truck, one of the officers told me that Janet continued screaming and struggling until she wore herself out or until she was sedated. Most of the times the police came to take Janet, they were trying to save her from freezing or from stormy weather. Other times neighbors and passers-by complained about her occasional nudity and wanted her gone. For some reason, though, she was able to spend most of her time in the park for many years.

Someone always came to the shelter to redeem the Louise on Janet's behalf, either a social worker or someone sent by her lawyer. Janet had family, but they had given up on her, according to one of the police officers who picked her up most often. He told me what he knew of her story.

Janet once had a normal family and a normal life. She had two children who lived somewhere back east. She also had a reasonable income from somewhere, besides her Social Security. No one knew what precipitated her move to the park. She had a lawyer who took care of her finances. He and her state-assigned social worker made sure she had whatever she would accept in the way of assistance. She even had a little apartment somewhere. The problem was that Janet was totally phobic about being indoors. She wouldn't go to shelters. She wouldn't go into her apartment. She refused medication. She wouldn't talk to doctors. Mostly she didn't talk to anyone, but she was able to make her wishes known when she wanted. She wasn't the kind of crazy who needed to be locked away. Janet's phobia extended to wearing clothing, especially in the summer, but after she was picked up a few times for indecent exposure, she made an attempt to stay covered when she thought someone might be watching. Someone provided her with those slip-over dresses she wore—the lawyer, the social worker or maybe some other concerned citizen.

When the weather got bad enough that Janet clearly became a danger to herself by remaining outdoors, her lawyer arranged for her to be involuntarily committed, but eventually she showed up in the park again with her dog. Sometimes she was gone for weeks and sometimes months, but she had been coming back to the park for five years or more when I first met her. I waved to her whenever I was in the neighborhood and picked up Louise two or three times a year for six years. Louise was getting arthritic when I last saw the two of them. Janet seemed to be doing okay. I hoped that Louise would live a long life. I was told that before she got the big shepherd, Janet had another big dog. Days after the other dog died, Louise showed up—a young dog, a spayed female, too well-behaved and well-bred to be a random dog-off-the-street. One of her guardians must have arranged for Janet to have another dog. Janet and Louise were still in residence at the park when I left Animal Control.

The other homeless person I got to know called himself Rupert Hilarity. He was well over six feet tall, long and thin, and wore long, light brown dreadlocks. Rupert couldn't make eye contact. When we talked, he held his hands near his face as if he might have to cover his eyes or defend himself. He kept his head turned away from anyone he spoke to. He had a shopping cart full of belongings that stayed with him and a tent hidden somewhere with the rest of his estate (as he put it).

When I first met Rupert, he had two dogs. They were medium-sized spotted mixed breeds that went almost everywhere with him. Sometimes he was allowed to tie them near a church or in the parking lot of a friendly business, if he had an errand to run that didn't allow for dogs. He always asked permission when he left his animals somewhere. I knew him and his dogs by sight long before I spoke to him.

People were always calling with complaints about street people with dogs, thinking the dogs must be neglected or mistreated somehow. I found that the dogs belonging to homeless people were exceptionally well-behaved and well-fed. They were well-loved. The dogs, by necessity, had to be calm around all kinds of people. They were with their masters twenty-four hours a day, learning to behave in harmony with the lifestyle. If they had to be tied up somewhere, they didn't bark or fuss, because if they did, they would be impounded or dog and owner would be ostracized.

Rupert and his two dogs acquired their share of complaints. We were supposed to check out the complaints, but Rupert wasn't easy to find. He walked all over the city. The first time I met him, a complaint had been made that his dogs were tied up in a church parking lot and were being a nuisance. When I got to the parking lot, the dogs were still there. The complainant said the dogs were barking and menacing people. I saw nothing of that behavior when I approached them. They were friendly, well-behaved and quiet—and they were on private property.

Rupert must have seen me approach his dogs because he came running across the lot. I told him about the complaint. He was polite in a courtly sort of way, although his manner of speech was odd and his body language was odder. Behind his raised hands, he thanked me for the information about the complaint. He had permission from the church custodian to leave the dogs where they were. "My dogs do not bark. Do not bark. They love but people don't love me. It's me they don't love. They use my dogs, my dogs, my dogs as an excuse." He was lucid and friendly but he seemed shy. He wasn't someone who blended in, even with other homeless people. His height and his hair made him easy to recognize. A few times I met with him, he spoke in word salads, making no sense, but he was always mild and polite, strangely poetic: "The lemon crickets look and your eyes are so loud. Melodies don't speak...leave my dogs, please."

One time, Rupert's dogs were picked up by another Animal Control Officer in the parking lot of a business, after someone called in another complaint, this time about "vicious dogs." According to Mitch, the officer who had picked up the dogs, they didn't bark at all when he approached them. They were totally mellow and cooperative and happy to go for a ride. Rupert wasn't around and the upset citizen was, so Mitch picked up the dogs. They were on a public right of way in front of a row of small businesses and they weren't wearing licenses or identification.

Rupert was incensed that Animal Control had picked

up the dogs when he had permission from a business owner for the dogs to be tied where they were. Whoever gave the permission didn't have authority over that little square of real estate. Rupert couldn't tolerate being inside the animal shelter. He couldn't visit his dogs when they were impounded. He stayed outside talking to himself and bemoaning the fact that his dogs were inside but he didn't approach anyone. He didn't ask for anything. Before the dogs had reached the three-day limit for strays, someone redeemed them for him. I wasn't around for the reunion with his dogs, but witnesses said Rupert was extremely emotional, so much so that he drew a small crowd, which he hated. He tied the dogs to his shopping cart and ran down the street, away from people. One of the kennel attendants said he looked like Ichabod Crane with dreadlocks running down the street pushing the cart, with his dogs flying along beside him.

Rupert and I developed a more personal relationship after one of his dogs became mother to six puppies. When the puppies were old enough, Rupert tied them to the cart in a long line— one pup tied to the mother and the next tied to the first pup and so on, a chain of puppies. The other adult dog, another female, was attached to the other side of the cart. The whole effect was hilarious, living up to Rupert's branding of himself, but the parade of puppies came to the attention of too many people who called Animal Control to complain. Usually people complained about possible cruelty, but the puppies were well cared for. Rupert walked all over town with them. Pinpointing his location was never easy. After more than two weeks of complaint calls from all over the city, I finally received a call that the dogs, the cart and the puppies were tied to a fence rail adjacent to the parking lot of a church in the Ballard neighborhood.

JANET AND RUPERT

Rupert was walking along the street when I came along. I rolled down my window to let him know I needed to talk to him. The fat little puppies entertained me while I waited for their keeper. The adult dogs were licensed now, and the puppies were all fat and healthy and too young to require licensing. After I reassured Rupert that I wasn't there to take his dogs, we had a talk about the complaints people were calling in. I suggested that he keep a low profile—as if that were really possible—and not let the puppies run along with him. They were getting too big to keep in the cart. Soon they would be too old to keep. He had to try to keep them out of sight until he could find homes for them.

"Find homes? They're Jessie's. She would be so sad. No no no no no no."

We talked for another half hour about what would happen when the puppies got older. They would have to be licensed. The law allowed a maximum of only three dogs—actually that's a stretch from "three dogs per household." Feeding all of them would be expensive. People would keep complaining and sooner or later—probably sooner—Animal Control would have to impound them. I assured him that Jessie wouldn't mind if her offspring went to good homes. Our conversation was relatively coherent, although he went off on tangents describing how things should be. I couldn't keep up with his long descriptions of his visions—for the puppies (basically, to remain with their loving families...), for dogs in general (no licenses, no cars...), for the world (nicer, much nicer and nicer...), for the complainers (who should go away to someplace they liked, like China or Tacoma...). I tried to steer the conversation toward practical reality. When he agreed that he should look for good homes for the puppies, I figured my job was done for the moment.

Two weeks after our conversation, someone stole four of Jessie's puppies and surrendered them to Animal Control as strays. Rupert was frantic. At the time, I was working the dispatch desk from 7:00 pm until 10:00 pm every night. Dispatch was on the second floor of the Animal Control shelter. The second floor was at the same level as the sidewalk. The shelter down below closed its doors to the public at 5:00 pm, but dispatch continued to operate in the upstairs office until the police dispatcher took over animal calls from 10:00 pm until 7:00 am.

On the day that the puppies were surrendered, Rupert came and stayed near the shelter, but he couldn't make himself come inside during business hours. Instead, he waited until after dark and then pounded on the door to the upstairs offices. He continued pounding until I opened the door. I could see him through the small one-way window in the door. He was frantic, incoherent, but still deferential, speaking unintelligible sentences faster that I could follow. At first, I thought he was in one of his word salad episodes, but as he calmed down and slowed down, I understood that he was asking—begging, pleading—to see the puppies. He told me that someone had stolen them from the box where he had been keeping them since I told him he couldn't let them walk around in public. He had found homes for two of them. He was working on finding homes for the four remaining pups when a mean woman came to yell at him about keeping them in the box. She scooped up all four and put them in her car and told him she was taking them to the animal shelter. She wouldn't listen. He couldn't/wouldn't stop her.

I couldn't let him inside to visit his puppies after hours and he didn't have the means to get them out of impound. Even if he had the money, he would only be able to take one of them, since he already had two licensed dogs. All I could do was promise that I would look out for them. I agreed that we would give them extra days to be adopted. I knew the kennel staff would be okay with that. They sympathized with Rupert. The puppies were cute and healthy, but plenty of cute and healthy pups were euthanized every day.

Rupert's pups were special cases. Everyone in the shelter was on Rupert's side. He came back every night for the next week, always asking to see the puppies and always being told I couldn't let him in. If he really wanted to see them, he had to go into the shelter during working hours. Once we got that out of the way, he wanted to talk about his dogs. He wouldn't answer questions about himself. I had work to do and I couldn't spend much time with him, but we talked for a few minutes every night until all the puppies had been adopted. He was a sweet, funny, gentle man who lived for his dogs. As far as I know, nobody knew him except his dogs. No one knew his real name. When asked where he came from, he said "Nowhere," and that's the only non-dog-related question I ever heard him answer. Eventually he disappeared from the landscape. By the time I realized I hadn't seen him in a long time, I couldn't remember the last time I'd seen him. No one else knew what had happened to him, but we decided that he must have gone south to find an easier climate for outdoor living. At least that's what we hoped for him.

CHAPTER 24

THE BIG SHEEP

Bringing home a wild animal is not a good idea. People try to make all kinds of animals into pets, but usually wild is not a good idea. For instance, someone took home a bighorn sheep sometime in the early 1980s, probably when it was a baby. Maybe the person was a hunter who killed the baby's mother. Maybe some idiot decided to go out and capture a baby sheep on a dare. Maybe a baby bighorn followed a mountain climber home. However, it happened, taking home a bighorn sheep was illegal as well as a bad idea.

Animal Control received a call to pick up a "large goat" tied to a dumpster in the parking lot of an apartment building. The call was assigned to me and I went to the relatively isolated apartment building at the south end of town, where I found a bighorn sheep tied to the dumpster. The animal was a lot bigger than a goat or a domestic sheep—more the size of a small horse, with huge curved horns. His coat was brown, soft to the touch. I thought his coat would be stiff and straight, like a horse's summer coat, but it was much softer, woollier—like a sheep. He had white stripes at his shoulders and white patches around his nose and cheeks. His rear end looked as if someone had used a salad bowl as a measure to paint a big circle of white around his small tuft of a tail. I suppose the white helps the bighorns keep track of one another on mountain paths. All in all, he was spectacularly gorgeous and seemed docile as a lamb.

The big parking lot was deserted, except for a few cars parked near the building. The dumpster sat far away from the building. The person who made the call to Animal Control didn't leave a name, and no one came out to greet me or give any information about my new friend. Someone had looped a thin, frayed rope about five feet long around the animal's neck. The knot at the dumpster end was too tight for me to undo, and the rope didn't look strong enough to keep the bighorn secured if he wanted to pull away. I decided to tie a braided nylon leash around his neck and clip a second leash to the first one before cutting the rope. My truck had a supply of braided nylon leashes which came in handy for more than moving dogs.

The dumpster was smelly. The sheep and I moved over to my truck, where I tied him to the passenger door. I had to reach above my head to hold his horn so I could steer him to the truck. Steering a bighorn sheep by holding its horn is a strange thing to be doing on a sunny afternoon. I felt lucky to be able to be so close to the amazing creature and once again thanked the gods for my job, but then I had to figure out what to do with him. He wouldn't fit into the truck. I called the dispatcher to let him know what I had found and to ask if he had any ideas about what to do with the beast. He said he would get back to me.

Sheep and I spent the rest of the afternoon doing very little. The dispatcher kept checking in to let me know he was still working on transport. I pulled some grass and weeds to see if Sheep was hungry. He was. Around the edges of the parking lot were more weeds and grass for gathering. He ate what I collected while I ate my lunch. I sat in the passenger seat of the truck with the window open, which placed Sheep's nose near eye level. He was not particularly curious about anything. He chewed. He liked to be rubbed on his forehead and his pretty amber eyes stared at me vacantly most of the time. Ordinary sheep aren't known for their intellects. Extraordinary sheep must be the same.

Eventually the dispatcher got back to me and said that a wild animal park would take the sheep to evaluate for their collection of animals. They were located about an hour and a half south of the city. No one was available to pick up the animal until the following day. I asked what was going to be done about the bighorn sheep's immediate needs, and mine. The dispatcher said he would get back to me. I didn't mind working a little overtime, but neither Sheep nor I was interested in spending the night in a parking lot.

My shift ended at 7:00 pm. At 5:30 pm, Sheep and I had been waiting over two hours for some travel assistance. Finally, one of the shift supervisors, Teddy, who was not working that day, called to let me know he was coming to pick up Sheep as soon as he could get his horse trailer hooked up. He arrived around 6:45 pm. Sheep walked into the trailer with no problem.

Teddy asked me, "Where did they say to take him?"

"Where did who say to take him?"

"Where are we going? Who is keeping this thing overnight?"

"He's not a thing and nobody said anything to me about where he's going. I thought someone must have told you before they sent you out here."

"Nope."

"Got any suggestions?"

"I can't take him home. My horses would freak out."

"Let's take him to the shelter. One of the kennels is big enough to hold him and he's not hard to handle. I'll follow you and help you unload him."

We drove about 15 miles to the animal shelter. After I parked my truck, I went around back and opened the gate to the loading area for Teddy to pull his truck in. We could hear the dogs barking. Sheep could also hear the dogs barking. He was moving around nervously in the trailer. Teddy unhooked both sides of the back door and we lowered the door to the ground, to provide the ramp for Sheep's exit. Teddy walked up the ramp to get next to the bighorn's head so he could guide him backwards. As soon as Teddy was close enough, Sheep kicked out with a front foot, hitting Teddy's left arm and pushing him into the side of the trailer. His yell brought the dispatcher downstairs, and when Teddy had cautiously made his way out of the trailer, Bruce the dispatcher helped me lift and secure the back door of the trailer.

Teddy had a gash on his arm. "I think it might be broken. My own fault. Damn. My fault. Hey, Bruce, would you move the truck and trailer up the alley a ways? Keys are in it. Might make the sheep happier. He'll be in there until somebody picks him up."

"The least I can do is drive you to the ER."

"Yeah, thanks. The least is good enough. Should've known better. Wild animal. Unpredictable."

Teddy's arm was broken, but it healed in a few weeks. The bighorn sheep went to the wild animal park and lived happily ever after I imagine. I called to ask about him later that week. He was in quarantine but seemed to be in good health, too friendly with people, though. The Trek curators weren't sure he would integrate into their little herd, since he may not have seen his own kind for a while, but if he didn't like company, they would make other accommodations.

Making wild animals into pets is not a good idea. Our Sheep proved a point. He was much luckier than most. Not every city has a place nearby for displaced bighorn sheep and not everyone forgives a broken arm as easily as Teddy.

CHAPTER 25

SPIKE

I met some spectacular dogs during my years with Animal Control. One of them, Spike, was a wire-haired Ibizan Hound, one of the most unusual dogs who came to stay with me temporarily. Ibizans are sight-hounds, like Greyhounds. They are one of the oldest breeds, bred to sight and then run down their prey. I came to know Spike through a series of events involving the woman who was responsible for the first litter of wire-haired Ibizans born on the West Coast—maybe the first in the United States. Giselle's plan was to introduce wire-coated Ibizans to the U.S., breed them, and sell them. She went to an island in the Mediterranean to purchase a pair of wire-coated dogs for breeding. The wire coat is a recessive gene. Starting with two wire-hairs upped the chances that some of their pups would also have the wire coats.

Because of the laws about bringing these dogs to the United States, Giselle had to take the Ibizans first to Canada and then across the border into the U. S. The female was already pregnant. After Giselle and her dogs crossed the border from Vancouver, British Columbia, she stopped in Washington and decided to settle there for a while. She didn't have a more specific destination in mind. The Seattle area had some Ibizan fanciers who might be interested in the wire-hairs. She rented a little house on the west side of a steep hill, where the first litter of seven puppies was born.

Giselle had not considered how she would market her unusual dogs or how she would obtain enough money to show them. She barely had enough money to pay the rent and feed the pups and she hadn't yet made any contacts in Seattle.

When the puppies were about seven weeks old, their mother tunneled under a fence at the side of the house on the hill. The fence was adjacent to a six-foot-tall rock retaining wall. Mother dog was probably a bit tired of the seven pups by this time and wanted a break. She squeezed under the fence and jumped off the retaining wall into the yard next door with no problem. One of her puppies tried to follow. His attempt to jump down after Mom was less successful. He landed in a tangle of legs and broke his left rear leg.

Giselle called Animal Control just before 9:00 pm that night. I was filling in for the dispatcher and answered the phone. The woman on the other end of the line demanded that someone come right away to pick up an injured puppy that MUST be euthanized immediately. She sounded a little inebriated, as well as hysterical. I informed her of the $5.00 fee for picking up a surrendered animal and she screamed that she couldn't afford a "god damn five dollars," but this was an emergency and someone needed to come IMMEDIATELY. "This is a VERY valuable pure-bred animal and he's badly injured and I CAN'T TAKE A CHANCE THAT HE'LL GET INTO THE WRONG HANDS! He needs to be put out of his pain NOW!" I didn't ask for more information about the pup. I promised someone would be at her house as soon as possible. "NOW!" was her last word before I hung up.

The only other officer on duty was finishing up several

calls before his 11:00 pm quitting time. I was also due to quit at 11:00. At 9:00 pm dispatch was turned over to the city police. Animal Control took only emergency calls through the police dispatcher from 9:00 pm until 7:00 am when the day shift took over. I decided I would take this call and see what the big deal was about this puppy. I grabbed my set of keys and set off in my truck for the address she gave, which was about twenty minutes from the shelter and not too far from the night-time emergency veterinarian. I knew Dr. Ted well, having brought him dozens of injured animals. Before I left the shelter, I called to tell him I was bringing him another one, "some kind of valuable and exclusive pure-bred. Just a puppy. I'm not sure what he is or how bad he's injured, but his owner wants him put down. See you in a few minutes."

I rang the doorbell of Giselle's house and heard a chorus of barking. The dogs were locked in a back room, except for the most amazing looking puppy I had ever seen. Giselle came out on the porch and handed him to me. He was partially wrapped in a towel with legs sticking out everywhere. I didn't see any blood, but he squealed when she handed him over. "Here, take him. He has to be put down."

"Where's his injury?"

"Leg's broken, see there?" I saw some swelling of the pup's left rear leg. Not surprisingly, he cried out again when his leg moved a little as I held him. I tried to keep the leg as still as possible, which wasn't easy while holding him in a towel. He kept trying to move and was causing himself pain, which made all three of us more tense. He seemed to consist mostly of a head and many legs sticking out of the towel (although when I counted, he only had the usual four.). His torso under the towel felt too small for his head and extremities. His adorable, mostly white, very pointy puppy head had a diamond shaped reddish-brown spot on the crown. Two big ears, bent like wings, stuck out on either side of the spot. His big sad eyes were amber. "That's all? Just the leg?"

"Yes, that's all. I can't afford a vet and can't take chances someone'll breed him. He's too valuable. He HAS to be put down." Her breath smelled of alcohol. I wanted to get out of there. I also really didn't want this obviously fixable little creature killed.

"If you can't pay the five dollars, I'll take him as a stray. You won't have to sign anything or be responsible for the fee."

"Fine. Jus' take him and make sure he's euthanized. Right away. I don' want him to suffer any more." She started to cry.

"I'm heading to the emergency vet right now."

She went back into the house. I carried the puppy to the truck and put him in the front seat, being mindful of his injured leg. Every movement caused him pain. Aside from his horrible situation, he was a comical-looking little animal. And sweet. He was mostly white with reddish-brown patches. The wiry hair at the top of his head gave an indication of a natural mohawk. His mohawk was the first sign of the wire coat he would have as an adult. His ears made him looked a little like a sad rabbit. Even though he was comical, he also managed to look as if he came from canine royalty. I imagined he would grow into his ears and his long legs. He was shaped for speed, or at least he looked like he would eventually be, with the body-type of a racing hound. I tried to wrap the towel so his leg was immobilized as much as possible and drove as fast as traffic would allow to the only veterinarian in the city that was open twenty-four hours. Dr. Ted liked working the night-shift. "I'm not so good with people. Have to fix too many of their stupid mistakes." I liked him a lot.

"Hey, Officer, you got a winner here. Never treated one of these. He looks kind of like an Ibizan Hound. Never saw one with a coat like this. Put him down here so I can look at the leg." The doctor unwrapped the towel to look at the damage. "Let's try to get him splinted up before this place gets busy."

"The owner said she wanted him euthanized, but she gave him up as a stray. I don't think that gives her any legal standing over what happens to him."

"I wouldn't kill this animal for all the Wild Turkey in Tacoma. I'm going to splint this leg and give him back to you. You can decide what to do with him after that. Won't take too long."

"Okay. I'll take him home if you fix him up. I can take him to see Phyllis in the morning." Phyllis was Dr. B.'s wife, also a vet. She was the primary doc to my five live-in dogs and three live-in cats.

"Right. This dog is special. Find him a special place."

I took him home and called him Spike because of his budding punk look. Dr. Phyllis x-rayed his leg to make sure it was aligned properly and put a cast on it. When he was no longer in pain, he was an enthusiastic, awkward, charming little dog. By the time the leg healed, Spike was beginning to grow into an imposing, unusual dog-creature. My dogs taught him house manners, but he was way too interested in the cats. If any of them gave him the slightest encouragement, he chased them over the furniture and out the dog-door, where they escaped to the top of the fence. I did everything I could to curtail Spike's hobby, but he wouldn't give it up. The cats didn't seem to mind. When they were in the mood, they co-existed peacefully with him, but too often they got him into chase mode and nothing in the house was safe. My network of dog people was on alert to help find him a home, but he wasn't an ordinary dog and he needed an extraordinary home, somewhere that he would never be seen by Giselle. He was remarkable. He was memorable, and almost as tall as a Great Dane by the time he was six months old. His white coat was whiter than white. His large red patches were placed with an eye for exotic design. He smelled like flowers all the time. He never smelled like a dog. Out in the world everybody noticed him. I couldn't take him outside our fence for fear Giselle might hear about him. She may have given up her legal ownership of him, but I knew she could cause trouble. She might want him back. He really was too beautiful. Giselle's main concern seemed to be that he might be bred indiscriminately, so he was neutered as soon as he was old enough.

Every Sunday, I loaded all the current and permanent dogs in my van and went to visit my friend, Leonie. She was a professor at the University of Washington. Her field of study was genetics, but she preferred teaching pre-science classes to disadvantaged students. Research with fruit flies fell off her agenda. Affirmative action was in full swing at that time, and many of the students the University chose to fill the quotas had not had the educational advantages of other students who competed to get into the University. Leonie took those students under her wing. She created a science class that introduced students to concepts they would need to absorb to be successful in science classes and science majors. Her classes became so popular that a good number of the rest of the science majors wanted in, but she set an affirmative action quota of her own, which limited the number of non-affirmative action students to only a few. Her classes expanded until she was teaching two or three classes each quarter.

I met Leonie because she was a family friend of one of my friends. At the time I earned extra money doing miscellaneous odd jobs with skills learned through my eclectic education and through earlier employment experiences. Leonie hired me to help her with her huge garden, to build railings for her basement stairs, to add plexiglass doors to her bookshelves, and to house-sit when she traveled, along with a multitude of other small tasks. We became good friends.

Leonie loved my dogs. She built a chain link fence around the front of her house just for the dogs so I wouldn't have to leave them at home when I worked for her. Her property was about three-quarters of an acre in a section of the city where most of the houses were huge and had swimming pools rather than gardens. The house itself was a modest two-bedroom cottage with windows that would have overlooked Lake Washington if the back of her property hadn't been covered with evergreen trees. They were the last of the forest that had been cleared to build the neighboring houses. She refused to cut them down just for a view of the lake.

Eventually, the dogs and I went to Leonie's house every Sunday, whether I had work to do there or not. She baked popovers, golden and delicious with butter and strawberry jam. Other people came to popover Sundays—guests from out of town, colleagues, ex-students....Her guests were always interesting and we chatted about everything while drinking our tea or coffee, eating popovers and slipping bits to the dogs under the table—my five dogs, Spike and whatever other dogs came with their people to join us.

Leonie had two cats, but they didn't stick around for popovers. One spent most of his life outside. He was a ginger Tom with tattered ears who had invited himself to live with her. His job was to keep watch over the garden and he was called The Gardener. The other cat, a talkative Siamese named Becky arrived in my pocket (before popover Sundays began), a tiny stray from the Animal Control Shelter, too young to put up for adoption. Leonie adored her cats.

One Sunday an extraordinarily handsome Englishman came to eat popovers. Professor Hugh West taught Slavic languages at the University. Leonie invited him specifically to meet Spike. The professor had owned sight-hounds when he was a child living in Morocco. He told stories about them and Leonie thought he ought to meet Spike. By this time Spike was seven months old. He was a handful. He was bigger than anyone imagined he would be. He was big enough to take food from tables and counters while all four of his feet remained on the floor. His wire coat grew longer, making him look either distinguished or silly, depending on his mood. Taking him out in public was impossible. Every person we passed gawked at him or stopped to ask questions about him.

Hugh fell in love with Spike immediately. He called his wife to come over, but she was busy. The next week he came back to Leonie's with his wife, Diane, specifically to have her meet Spike. She was described to me by Leonie as a pipe-smoking, no-nonsense woman who was employed by a group of Quakers to work on projects promoting peace. She often wore a red bowler hat.

Diane was obviously a little irritated with Hugh when they first walked in the door. She was gorgeous enough to be a perfect match to her exceedingly handsome husband. She played down her beauty, however, by wearing a plaid flannel shirt and baggy gray slacks—no make-up. She was wearing the red bowler hat, no pipe. She and Hugh were as memorable a pair as Spike was memorable as a dog.

Hugh and Diane could have stepped out of a movie screen. They would have been a perfect couple to take the Orient Express with Sherlock Holmes and Agatha Christie. I could picture them in 18th century finery with the opulent background of the train's dining car, taking part in the murder mystery with Detective Poirot, chatting with the Princess....

At first Diane was not that impressed by Spike, but Hugh talked and wheedled a little and reminded her of the dogs of his youth. Spike was at his charming best for her. By the end of the last popover, I had agreed to deliver Spike to their house as soon as they had prepared the house to receive him, which included installing about a half mile of fencing around part of their five-acre property and installing a bigger dog door. They already had a female Viszla. The Viszla was about half as tall as Spike. She was a homebody and didn't need a fence to keep her close to home, but Spike's long legs could take him miles away in a few minutes. He needed an enclosure.

Three weeks later, I drove to Hugh and Diane's secluded home with a gated entry. The iron gate was open as Hugh had promised it would be. They asked me to close it after I had driven through, which I did. The driveway continued along a curving track that hid the house from view. When I arrived at the front of the house, they were there to greet me and to let Spike out of the car to check out his new play area. They told me that one acre of their five-acre property was now securely fenced. Most of the new six-foot chain link fence couldn't be seen through trees and greenery. A six-foot stone wall spanned the front of the property and part of the boundary at each side. After greeting Hugh and Diane briefly, Spike ran across the wide lawn, into the trees. He came back into view within a couple of minutes, but he continued to run around and around the huge yard. I had never seen him run free before. My yard was big for a city house, a corner lot, but it was not big enough for Spike to stretch his legs and really run. He was so beautiful he brought tears to my eyes.

Hugh and Diane were as affected as I was, watching Spike's joyful, effortless, flying gallop. The extraordinary dog had his extraordinary home and I had new friends, who had made chocolate croissants to eat at the table on their vine-covered porch. Sasha the Viszla came out to the porch at Diane's invitation. Sasha watched the strange dog for a minute before she ran out to greet him. They made a few perfunctory sniffs of introduction and then Sasha joined her new sibling, running and playing until they wore themselves out. Eventually they came back to the porch and both flopped onto the big dog bed that had formerly been Sasha's alone. She shared it willingly with her new partner. Spike's move to his permanent home went without a hitch.

CHAPTER 26

LUNA FLOR

After I met the Ibizan puppy, Spike, and after Spike had gone to his new home, I wanted to find out more about the Ibizan breed. I looked up activities where Ibizans might be found and discovered "lure coursing." This is a sighthound competition in which the lure, a scented piece of fur, is carried around on a track laid in an open field, and two or three dogs at a time race after it—a little like racing greyhounds, but on a much smaller and more primitive scale. I decided to go to a lure coursing competition and watch the dogs pretend to do what they were bred to do—run down their prey. In this competition, they never caught the lure, but the fun was in the chase.

About twenty dogs were at the competition, including four wire-haired Ibizans, Spike's siblings. Giselle was there, looking sharp in her sporting clothes, complete with cashmere scarf and matching beret. I hoped she wouldn't recognize me and she didn't. While I was talking with one of the dog owners, telling him I was intrigued by the breed, Giselle came over and introduced herself. She pointed at the course and said we should watch her dogs race. Two of her dogs were lined up along with a smooth coated Ibizan. A bell rang and they were off.

The course was a huge irregular track in a field of tall

grasses, and the dogs were not always easy to see. When they were about three-quarters of the way around the track, the dog in the lead suddenly jumped up high above the grass, turned around in mid-air and came down with her rear end up and her front feet straight in front of her, in the recognizable "let's play" position. Everyone on the side-lines laughed except Giselle. The other two dogs were only interested in the lure and passed by the playful dog without acknowledging the invitation. The playful one followed the other two to the finish, after having been in the lead for most of the race and she came in third. "That bitch, she and I don't get along. These are regal animals, don't you think? That one is a ridiculous clown."

My response to the dog's antics was a little different. I thought she was great—and hilarious. "I don't know. I like a dog with a sense of humor."

"Well, she's got that, I suppose. She's not show quality, and she won't excel at coursing. My other dogs are only eleven months old and three of them are already on the way to championships in the show ring. I left my best male at home. He's going to sire some spectacular pups." I thought a little sadly about the pups Spike would never sire.

I followed Giselle over to ringside where she took possession of her two dogs and their ribbons—a blue ribbon for the win, and a third-place green for the silly bitch. "What's the silly bitch's name?"

"Luna Flor. Moon Flower. Such a lovely name, wasted on this wispy idiot. Look, her coat is almost smooth, but not smooth enough, and not wiry enough either."

"What are you going to do with her?"

"I don't know. I'd give her to anybody for $100. It'll cost that to get her spayed, and I won't let her out of my sight until that's done. She's not breeding quality."

"Will you take a check?"

"You're kidding."

"Not kidding. I really like her. I came here because I like the breed, but I only want a pet. My dogs don't do anything much except make me happy. And this one is definitely entertaining."

"How many dogs do you have?"

"It varies. I do a lot of fostering. My keepers are a German Short Hair, an AmStaff and a little mutt that looks like a miniature Corgi. I have a secure, fenced yard and plenty of dog-amenities."

"You really want this dog? She has some annoying habits. She barks. She gets into garbage."

"Yeah, dogs do that. I can cope. My dogs and I can get her back on the straight and narrow."

"I'll take a check. She'll go to my vet to get spayed as soon as I can get an appointment. Where do you live?"

"Ballard, in the city."

"I'm not too far. You can pick her up in about a week. Here's my card."

I made out the check. The next week Giselle called me and said I could pick up Luna. I retrieved her from the house where I had picked up Spike months before. Luna was still wearing the funnel collar that kept her from licking the stitches in her belly.

Luna settled in perfectly, and I was excited to be able to tell my popover Sunday group and Professor West about the new addition to the pack. Miss Luna was sweet, calm, friendly, funny and charmingly exotic. I couldn't go anywhere without having people approach me wanting to ask questions about her, but she didn't have to remain a secret. She wasn't my first impulse buy, but she was a bargain. She smelled like flowers, too, just like her brother Spike.

I didn't stay in touch with Giselle. I saw her at dog shows and lure coursing events occasionally. Luna enjoyed running after the lure, even though she was easily distracted. She collected two red ribbons before we gave up the sport.

Giselle heard rumors of another wire-haired Ibizan seen around town. She suspected it might be her surrendered puppy and complained in writing to Animal Control. The AC manager wrote back saying that the records showed her surrendered stray was taken to the emergency vet and was never in the shelter. That was all the record said. Spike was a stray with no paper trail.

Luna was always a hit at popover Sundays. Visitors were fascinated with her, and she with them. She stayed with me for almost fourteen years. Soon after Luna came to stay, I brought home a little terrier mix with a badly healed broken leg. Tino looked like a miniature version of Robert Reddog. He completed my pack.

CHAPTER 27

ALWAYS A DOWNSIDE

Working as an Animal Control Officer, I woke up every morning happy to be heading off to work, but some work experiences were not as fun as others. Some experiences I would rather not remember, but of course bad experiences happened, too. The truth is, horrific things happened, the kinds of things that are obvious parts of being an Animal Control Officer—the kinds of things that are witnessed by many people who dedicate their working lives to animals. I was a public servant. The cruelest animals, the ones capable of the most senseless acts are my own species.

Even though I stopped having to participate in the euthanizing of unwanted animals after I had been at the job for two years, I still knew it was happening every day. Even though I wanted people to want pets, too many people didn't deserve to have them and too many people did stupid, cruel or ignorant things with animals that made me wish that I didn't wish I owned a cattle prod or some such other non-lethal form of immediate punishment. I fantasized about being able to say, "You idiot! What were you thinking?" And then ZZZZTTT.

Dealing with humans was the worst part of my job. In the winter, I always had to pick up some Doberman or other short-haired "watch dog" that had frozen to death in its dog house or out in the yard on a chain. I could issue citations for cruelty, but the kinds of people who do such things—usually out of ignorance or sheer drug-induced stupidity rather than malice—can ignore citations as easily as they ignore their pets and children.

On one of my calls, Child Welfare Services had to be contacted because a little boy in diapers, barely able to walk, was on the front porch of an apartment where I went because of a dog complaint. When I started to knock on the door, he panicked and said, "No! No! Mommy s'eeping!" I knocked some more. Mommy never answered the door. I called the police and they contacted Child Welfare Services when they received no useful response from the boy's mother. I stayed with the damp, messy sad little boy for more than an hour before someone from Child Welfare showed up to take him to safety. I never saw or heard a dog near the apartment. Mommy wouldn't even answer the door for the loud pounding of the police, although they got her to say "Go away," confirming she wasn't dead or comatose. They were able to inform her that her son was being removed from her care. Still, she didn't open the door. ZZZZTTT.

A couple of times I picked up baby pigs—not piglets. These were pigs barely small enough to pick up, but more than twice as big as a bread box. My first pig was the result of someone leaving the animal in a friend's yard as an April Fool's joke. Ha ha. Another time the pig was a prank birthday gift.

Pigs scream. Squeal isn't a big enough word to describe the noise made by a little pig under stress. They scream louder than banshees when they are picked up against their will, and they have some mad skills at avoiding capture. I refused to chase the piggies, but had to accept custody of them and take them to the man who contracted with AC to deal with farm animals. I don't know what he did with them, but I'm fairly certain the little pigs ended up as they were originally intended—as pork chops. I'm not a vegetarian, but I don't eat pigs, mostly for the same reasons I don't eat dogs. They are intelligent, social animals--and I promised a woman who rescues pigs that I would forego eating them. I saw around 80 of her pigs living happily on their acreage, hanging out in their friendship groups, (which they keep for a lifetime), and I now find pork as repugnant as dog meat or horse meat. Still, I eat cows and chickens, but I imagine the time might come when I meet a loved and loveable cow or chicken and change my mind. Right now I just thank them for their sacrifice. And I believe that all animals deserve respect and shouldn't be used as pranks. ZZZZTTT.

Another sickening bit of heartbreak happened the day I picked up a pit bull that weighed 30 pounds from some people (I use the word loosely) who had gone on a several-week bender—or vacation as they put it. They had no idea how somebody's dog got into their basement—with its empty dishes. The dog would have weighed 60 or 70 pounds at its normal weight. It wasn't able to walk. I carried it under one arm, as it wagged its tail and tried to lick my face. ZZZZTTT ZZZZTTT.

We also picked up dead animals. That wasn't pleasant, and sometimes it was gruesome, but dead things are dead and empty of life, usually. I picked up animals killed by neglect and a few animals killed accidentally—dog in hot-tub or cat in the dryer. Horrible incidents, horrible accidents. The neglectful humans surely deserved a ZZZZTTT, but I still ache for the people whose pets met accidental death under unforeseen circumstances.

I said that usually the dead animals we picked up off the street were empty of life. On one occasion that wasn't quite true. I picked up an unconscious raccoon from the middle of a residential street thinking it was dead. It wasn't. When I opened the door at the back of my truck to unload it, the raccoon and I almost gave each other heart attacks. The animal had no idea what was going on, having been unconscious before being caged. I slammed the door on its cute but soon-to-be-angry face. Raccoons are dangerous, although mostly they leave humans alone if we leave them alone. I called Eric from the wildlife rescue organization north of Seattle and slowed down my heart beat while I waited for him to arrive.

Eric was an animal whisperer. He wasn't much of a conversationalist, but he could calm and handle wild animals almost magically. He had only a blanket in hand when he opened the cage door. He slowly opened the cage door—it seemed he was moving slowly, but he had to be quick to grab the raccoon after opening the door. He enveloped the 30-pound-plus freaked-out animal in the blanket and gently carried it to his car. The raccoon didn't seem to be struggling while he carried it. He did what my friend Becky had done with that pigeon on my porch, but a raccoon is generally not as docile as a pigeon. By the time Eric unloaded the raccoon into the cage in his car, it was relatively calm and cooperative.

I only watched Eric in action a couple of times, once with the raccoon and once with an injured mother possum with a pouchful of babies. He handled injured raccoons, possums, foxes, seals, as if they were house pets, and they all appeared to respond to him as if they were house pets, according to stories told about him. The little rehabilitation center where he worked, called PAWS, has since grown into a large enterprise with multiple locations and services for the benefit of all kinds of animals, wild and domestic. Some humans are exceptionally good with and for animals.

With a few exceptions, people were usually the real problem on the calls regarding problem animals that I responded to. Police often had their guns out when I was picking up a barking dog at midnight, left alone, tied up in a back yard. Or when I had to tend to a defensive injured animal holding up traffic. I didn't mind those guns. The ones I minded were in the hands of curmudgeons who liked to discourage "dog-catchers" from coming onto their property or into their neighborhood. Having a gun pointed at me was completely effective in making me go away. Forget the ZZZZTTT. I was out of there. I could only hope that karma would give those ungentlemen a good ZZZZTTT.

Speaking of police, almost all of the police officers I worked with were the admirable men and women in blue. They were polite and sometimes helpful and sometimes funny. They appreciated having assistance with animal calls. Some officers I got to know a little, especially some on the night-shift, and I found them to be seriously dedicated to their duty to protect and serve.

One police officer, however, could not be called admirable. His neighbors kept complaining about his dog, which was chained in his front yard on a chain long enough to allow the dog to go into the yards of the neighbors on either side of his house. The dog could almost make it down to the sidewalk, but the house had two tiers of steps leading up to it with a wide landing in between. The very large Malamute mix was still three steps from the sidewalk at the end of his chain, still on private property. The dog was not unfriendly, but it barked at people who came by. Big barking dogs are scary. This one also preferred to use the neighbors' lawns for its toilette.

I never spoke to the owner of the problem dog in person. Twice notices were put on his door saying that he needed to reel in his dog. He called the shelter after the second notice and asked to speak to me. When I returned his call, he said all the wrong things, after identifying himself as a city police officer. He made it clear that he wouldn't make the dog's chain shorter, wouldn't pick up after the dog, etc. He said his neighbors were lucky to have him living next door to them (??). "You're supposed to be a member of the force, Lady. If you don't back me up then I'll treat you the same. Better be looking over your shoulder." It occurred to me that contacting his superior might make the situation worse. Police officers often defend their own even when their own don't necessarily deserve to be defended.

This officer's neighbors were advised that their only recourse was to sue him. They had already tried contacting his chief, but the chief said to call Animal Control. That would be me. I talked to my supervisor. He said that we had no grounds to issue a ticket under the city's animal control laws. The dog wasn't loose. It wasn't vicious, in spite of its tendency to bark. The police would have to determine if we should impound it for being a noise nuisance. Not likely. The dog was a big, playful, otherwise well-cared-for, lonesome animal. He wasn't the real problem. As with so many "problem dogs," the owner was the problem. ZZZZTTT.

In the following six months, I received two traffic tickets while driving my own car. One ticket was for not coming to a complete stop at a stop sign (we used to call those almost-stops "California stops") and the other ticket was for going seven miles over the 35-mph speed limit on a wide, empty road in the warehouse district on a sunny day. A third officer pulled me over to give me a warning about a small stuffed animal on the ledge behind the back seat.

"It's a hazard. Blocks the view of traffic behind you. Move it."

"Yes, sir. I'll move it."

"See that you do."

Maybe the tickets were deserved. Prevalent as "California stops" were (and are), they were and are still illegal, but I had never heard of anyone getting more than a warning for an "almost-stop." Seven miles over the speed limit seemed like too small an infraction for an expensive ticket. As for the stuffed dog on the ledge, people used to have whole dioramas, knick-knacks, boxes, families of stuffed things, small children (in an age before car-seats were mandatory) on that ledge behind the back seat that doesn't exist anymore in most newer cars. I went to court to contest both of the tickets and both were dismissed. Maybe they had nothing to do with that officer with the dog and the bad attitude. Maybe they did. I think they did. No part of the experience gave me a more benevolent view of the general public. ZZZZTTT? Maybe.

Lastly come the citizens who thought they were going to save a dog from the evil dog-catcher. This was a small terrier running alongside a busy non-residential highway. Several people called about it. I went to see if I could at least herd it away from the roadway. Frightened dogs are all but impossible to catch in a situation like this one. I pulled over to the side of the road well ahead of the running dog, prepared to guide it into a landscaped area that opened onto residential streets about 100 feet down a hill. Unfortunately for the animal, and for me, a couple of concerned citizens stopped to save the dog from the dogcatcher. They chased it—"Noooooooo!" I tried to wave them away. Predictably it ran into traffic and was immediately struck by a car. These people received their immediate punishment in the result of their misguided actions. They left the scene as soon as they saw what they had done. The dog was dead on impact. I loaded the little body into my truck and called the owners. Their phone number was on the dog's ID tag.

CHAPTER 28

THE PRISON PET PARTNERSHIP PROGRAM AT PURDY

I had been working for Animal Control for about five years when a friend introduced me to the Prison Pet Partnership Program at Purdy. Marilyn was a dog person I met while attending dog events—shows, rallies, competitions. She had three standard poodles—a white one, a black one and a brown one—along with a pug and a Dalmatian, and she was immersed to the point of obsession in training her animals.

Marilyn approached me because of my Ibizan Hound, Luna, who always attracted attention, wherever I went. Marilyn and I became good friends after she invited me and my dogs to attend a birthday party—for a dog—which included seventeen well-behaved dogs belonging to other guests, three of my five, and Marilyn's poodles. Dogs outnumbered human guests. Luna stole a single slice of roast beef from the buffet table, but she did it so daintily, without touching anything more than the slice she was after, and without putting her paws on the table, that everyone said "aww" and let her get away with it.

While the dogs played at the party, Marilyn and I talked about her volunteer work at the Prison Pet Partnership Program at Purdy. The prison program was at the Washington State women's prison at Purdy, a tiny town near Gig Harbor, Washington, which is about 12 miles north of Tacoma. The whole idea was amazing, a little surreal and fascinating.

I wanted to volunteer at the prison program too, of course, but I had no idea how I could help out. Marilyn said I knew plenty about dogs if I worked at Animal Control. She said she knew they would find me something to do, if I really wanted to drive all the way to Purdy on a regular basis. Purdy was on the opposite side of Puget Sound from Seattle. I could get there by taking an hour-long ferry ride to Bremerton and driving another 20 miles south, or by driving to Tacoma to cross the Tacoma Narrows Bridge and then north to Purdy, more than 60 miles from my home, in unpredictable, usually messy traffic. The Narrows Bridge was notorious for traffic jams. I was definitely up for the trip. We made a date to go out to the prison. Marilyn took her poodles and I took my pit bull, Robert Reddog, along with Luna. At first, I was hesitant about taking a pit bull to a prison but Marilyn thought he would be fine. "He's going to be a big hit with the girls," she said, and he was. Everybody inside loved him.

I met Dawn and Marsha, the two dog trainers who had built the original idea for a class in dog training into an amazingly successful educational program, in spite of naysayers. Dawn noticed that I drove a cargo van. She immediately gave me a job. I began going with the program's veterinarian to the local Humane Society to choose dogs for the inmates to train. The vet did a physical exam and then we tested the dogs' temperaments for suitability for training. The dogs needed to be relatively calm, young, not prone to biting or chronic barking, and amenable to training. I spent all my free time working with the program, doing errands, transporting dogs, watching my own dogs being used as training guinea pigs, assisting with paperwork, assisting with challenging grooming projects. Some of the animals we chose required hours of patient de-matting, clipping and shaping. The inmates relished the task.

The PPP program was five years old when I signed on as a volunteer. The inmate students were running two businesses, a boarding kennel and a grooming salon. The kennel building that had originally been intended to house program dogs was largely empty until the boarding business evolved. Dawn and Marsha and the students figured out within a few months that the dogs learned more quickly if they spent 24-hours a day with their trainers. The inmates loved having dogs with them all day long. At the end of a four to six-month training period, they had to give up the dogs to members of the public who had applied to receive a dog from the program. Graduations in the prison gym were dramatic fests, where the dogs were ceremonially handed over to their new owners. Everybody cried and laughed and enjoyed the entertainment the inmates prepared to show off the dogs' abilities. Some of the people who received trained dogs stayed in touch with the program and the inmate-trainers, sending updates on the dog's status in their new homes.

In 1986, when I arrived as a volunteer at the Prison Pet Partnership, the Washington Corrections Center for Women housed about 150 women. In 1989 an effort was made to get rid of the program because the new director of education for the prison thought that dogs didn't belong in a prison. The first step was a requirement that the head of the PPP had to have a college degree. Neither Dawn nor Marsha had a college education although they had run the globally recognized program successfully for nine years. No one outside of the program knew it well enough to step into a leadership position. I resigned from my position as Animal Control Officer Two with only a small amount of regret and went to work at the PPP.

    The new education director continued to put pressure on the program and made impossible demands and changes. Eventually he succeeded in ending the first incarnation of the program. Although the original educational program run by Tacoma Community College was shut down, a global community supported a local group in creating a non-profit organization that continued to operate on the original model. Today the prison houses around 740 women. The Prison Pet Partnership Program continues. The twelve-run kennel is now a twenty-eight-run kennel. The program runs a popular boarding business, and inmates still have a grooming salon. They train animals taken from the Humane Society for the people from all over the country who apply to receive them. Miracles are still happening, and now animal programs flourish all over the world.

EPILOGUE

Leaving Animal Control when I did was the right thing to do. The job was more than rewarding, but it was also strenuous, both physically and mentally. The experience was worth every minute I spent in that brown uniform. I may not have quit the job if not for the prison program, but I left at the right time, before burnout and before cynicism. Animals are still my favorite people, but people have become a close second.

So many more moments come to mind from when I wore the uniform. I didn't mention the time that I helped a highway patrol officer catch ducklings in the middle of the interstate. He used his Smokey Bear hat to herd them and I captured them with the net that I never used before or after that roundup. We made the evening news on that occasion. And once my friend Al the zookeeper introduced me to two four-week-old tiger cubs. We played with them for a few minutes—extravagantly beautiful kittens with paws bigger than saucers. What an exceptional treat—unavailable on most life-trajectories.

Another time I made the news because of an animal was the day we released an elderly possum into Discovery Park. He had been found gnawing on car tires downtown, late one night. He toddled out of the cage onto one of the park's narrow paths through trees and thick greenery. He stayed on the path until he was out of sight. For some reason I picture him wearing tennis shoes, marching along down the center of the dirt path. He wasn't shod, of course, but memories can play tricks.

Sometime in 1986 I ran out of veteran's benefits and gathered together some of my college credits to collect a degree. I had the right configuration for a BA in English Literature. The degree allowed me to get hired at the prison program, although English Literature has little to do with animals or prisons. A degree of any kind opens paths. That pigeon set me on the right one initially, and since then, I've kept moving on, always with a dog or two or three at my side, to keep life interesting.

ABOUT THE AUTHOR

Linda Mack is happily retired, living in California with her partner, Charlene, and two fine dogs, Ralfie and Bubbles.

IMAGE CREDITS

Page 209—© Can Stock Photo/robertasch
Page 195—© Can Stock Photo/yod67
Page 191—© Can Stock Photo/Alinart
Page 181—© Shutterstock/TatyanaPanova
Page 175—© Can Stock Photo/vectorsun
Page 165—© Can Stock Photo/KevDraws
Page 159—© Can Stock Photo/gorovits
Page 149—© Can Stock Photo/Chetkova
Page 142—© Can Stock Photo/Chetkova
Page 135—© Can Stock Photo/arkela
Page 127—© Can Stock Photo/mehsumov
Page 119—© Can Stock Photo/alisher
Page 97—© Can Stock Photo/alisher
Page 91—© Can Stock Photo/iconisa
Page 69—© Can Stock Photo/EnkaParmur
Page 47—© Can Stock Photo/Jeane09
Page 43—© Can Stock Photo/Sudowoodo
Page 39—© Can Stock Photo/haris99
Page 35—© Can Stock Photo/Chetkova
Title Page/About the Author—© Can Stock Photo/alisher
Front Cover Cat—© Can Stock Photo/Sudowoodo

www.ingramcontent.com/pod-product-compliance
Lightning Source LLC
Chambersburg PA
CBHW061321040426
42444CB00011B/2719